Party Cakes

45 fabulous cakes for all occasions, with easy ideas for children's cakes

CAROL DEACON

NH
NEW
HOLLAND

First published in 2006 by
New Holland Publishers (UK) Ltd
London • Cape Town • Sydney • Auckland
www.newhollandpublishers.com

Garfield House
86–88 Edgware Road
London W2 2EA
United Kingdom

80 McKenzie Street
Cape Town 8001
South Africa

14 Aquatic Drive
Frenchs Forest
NSW 2086
Australia

218 Lake Road
Northcote
Auckland

Copyright ... Deacon
Copyrig... 2006

Copyrigh... K) Ltd
Ca... d

All rights ... , stored
in a retriev... lectronic,
mechani... pyright

ISBN-10: 1 84537 577 7
ISBN-13: 978 1 84537 577 5

Co-ordinating editor: Ruth Hamilton
Design: Paul Cooper, Helen Gibson and Kevin Kilbey
Cover design: Glyn Bridgewater
Photography: Edward Allwright
Production: Hazel Kirkman
Editors: Kate Latham, Gillian Haslam and Caroline Plaisted
Editorial Direction: Rosemary Wilkinson

Reproduction by Hirt & Carter Cape (Pty) Ltd and
Modern Age Repro House Ltd, Hong Kong
Printed and bound by Times Offset, Malaysia

ACKNOWLEDGEMENTS

The author and publishers would like to thank Renshaw Scott Ltd for
supplying sugarpaste, Cake Art Ltd and Culpitt Ltd for equipment, Guy, Paul
& Co Ltd for supplying vast numbers of cakeboards, Divertimenti for the
loan of the kitchen equipment and the Carlton Food Network News.

Carol Deacon would like to thank Tory Brettell, Kath Christensen, Sandy
Dale, Nicola Gill, Sally Hodgson, Chris Jones and Claire Stickland for their
unwavering support during various cake crises over the years, and Richard
Shelton for the use of his kitchen. Also Jack and Luke Aldridge-Deacon,
Natalie Allwright, Jemma Blake and Belinda Bellingham for all their help
and enthusiasm. Also a special mention to Joshua Pollins, one of her
youngest fans who will be tickled pink to see his name in print.

Important: In the recipes, use either metric or imperial measurements, but
never a combination of the two, as exact conversions are not always possible.
Every effort has been made to present clear and accurate instructions.
Therefore, the author and publishers can accept no liability for any injury,
illness or damage which may inadvertently be caused to the user whilst
following these instructions.

Contents

Introduction

First of all, let me say that this book would never have been put together had it not been for the important little people behind the scenes. I owe a debt of gratitude to my dedicated team of researchers, tasters and testers – Jemma, Belinda, Jack, Luke and Natalie (average age 6). They all worked tirelessly and without complaining (despite the vast amounts of chocolate and gingerbread that they had to consume in the line of duty) to prove that many of the designs in this book are so easy that even a child can make them. Thank you one and all. I hope the chocolate all washed out!

Because I realise that not all people are cake decorators by trade, I've tried to make things as foolproof as possible for you. The introduction section answers many of the basic questions about working with sugarpaste (rolled fondant) which I hope you'll find helpful. Then, with the cakes themselves, I have tried to cover as many occasions, interests and hobbies as I can, to make that annual dilemma of "What shall I make this year?" that little bit easier. I've given short cuts or alternatives wherever possible and even suggest where it is best to place the candles on your cake.

Some of the cakes are more of a challenge than others, but whether you're a child of six or sixty I hope you'll be inspired enough to pick up that rolling pin and get cracking!

Carol Deacon

Introduction to Sugarpaste (rolled fondant)

Throughout this book I have used one particular icing – sugarpaste. It is so versatile that it can be used to cover cakes and to create decorative models. You can pull it, roll it, stretch it, poke holes in it, colour it and, if in despair, scrunch it up and start again with it. It is so easy to use that even a child can work with it. All of the cakes in this book can be decorated with sugarpaste straight from the packet. You needn't add anything else apart from some colour and a lot of fun.

Here, I have answered the most common questions about working with sugarpaste and I hope that you enjoy making your own creations.

What is sugarpaste (rolled fondant)?

It's easy for people like me to assume that everyone knows what sugarpaste is. It's basically a mixture of icing (confectioners') sugar, glucose and egg white and is readily available in supermarkets and cake decoration equipment shops. It is also easy to make yourself (see recipe on page 19). The thing that confuses people most is its name, or perhaps I should say names. "Sugarpaste" is the term used in Britain and throughout this book. In the supermarket, you'll find it in the "home baking" section, next to marzipan. It could be lurking under one of its many pseudonyms such as "ready-to-roll icing", "fondant icing", "soft fondant", "rolled fondant", "edible modelling icing", "easy ice" and all sorts of other titles. Don't be daunted, or put off. They are all what we'd term "sugarpaste" and are all suitable to use for the designs in this book.

Some brands are available ready-coloured and some are even flavoured. Personally, apart from red and black sugarpaste which take a lot of food colour and physical energy to colour, I prefer to mix my own shades as I find some of the ready-coloured sugarpastes a little too soft for my liking. But, as with anything in life, the best way is to experiment with different brands to see which suits you best.

How do I use sugarpaste (rolled fondant)?
Keep it covered

There are a few basic rules that you need to follow when using sugarpaste. The first is that it dries out when exposed to the atmosphere, so you need to keep it covered when not in use.

When you buy it, it will come in blocks ranging from 250 g up to a 20 kg box. As soon as you cut open the packet and pull off the amount you need to use, reseal the packet or tightly wrap in a polythene bag. I buy rolls of small plastic freezer bags from the supermarket which I find ideal for storing all my bits of leftover icing. Then I place the bags into a large airtight plastic box and store it in a cupboard. Different colours should be kept in different bags to stop the colours from bleeding into one another.

Shop-bought sugarpaste has a shelf life of about eight months (check the side of the box as well). Home-made sugarpaste should be used up within a week. Neither type needs to be stored in a fridge.

Dust your surface

When using sugarpaste, always start by dusting your worksurface with icing (confectioners') sugar to prevent it sticking. Keep a small bowl of icing sugar handy all the time to dust your hands, utensils and surfaces. If you're in a humid kitchen or the air is damp, you will be surprised at how sticky your hands can get. Don't worry about any icing sugar smudges on the sugarpaste at this stage, they can be wiped away easily with a damp paintbrush when the cake is finished.

Treat it rough!

Begin by kneading the sugarpaste until it becomes nice and pliable. If it's quite cold in your kitchen then this may mean lots of physical exertion and liberal dustings of icing sugar. If you're trying to soften large quantities to cover a very large cake, break the icing up and knead it in small sections first. Then pile it all up and knead the whole thing together.

Some people prefer to microwave their sugarpaste for a few seconds to soften it but this does have its drawbacks. Apart from the risk of overheating the sugarpaste and possibly causing a nasty burn, microwaving can occasionally cause a skin to form on the surface of the sugarpaste. If it is then used to cover a cake it may crack on the edges and develop a crazy-paving appearance on the top and sides. This won't affect the taste of the icing but it will spoil the professional finish!

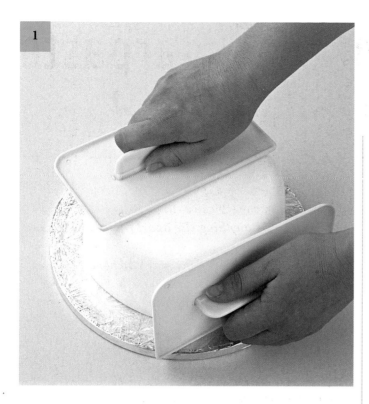

Will I need lots of special tools?

Not at all. Most of the equipment used in this book (see page 28), such as rolling pins, knives, drinking straws, paint and pastry brushes you will probably have already, which is why sugarpaste is such an excellent medium for the beginner to use. Where I have used something special such as a cutter, I have tried to suggest alternative methods as well.

If sugarcraft begins to get a grip on you, there are two pieces of equipment that I would recommend you to buy. The first is a turntable which really does make life easier. There are all types – plastic, metal, tilting, non-tilting, raised and flat. It's purely a question of taste and money as to which one you choose – I managed for years with a cheap flat one. You won't need one that tilts unless you're planning on venturing into the highly skilled world of royal icing.

The second piece of equipment that nobody could ever part me from are my cake smoothers (1). These are two pieces of flat plastic with a handle on the back. You hold them as you would an iron and run them over the sides and top of your covered cake to smooth out any lumps and bumps. These little beauties are what will lift your cake's appearance from that of the enthusiastic but probably lumpy-sided amateur to the smooth polished look of the professional. As a temporary measure, you can cut a couple of flat plastic sections out of the top of an ice cream or large margarine carton. They're a little more fiddly to use because you haven't got handles to grip but you can still use them to run around and smooth the top and sides. (See pages 21-22 for instructions on covering cakes and cake boards with sugarpaste.)

Both turntables and smoothers are available from cake decoration equipment shops and you may also find them in some kitchenware shops and department stores.

How do I colour sugarpaste (rolled fondant)?

The best products to use for colouring sugarpaste are food colour pastes. These have a thicker consistency than liquid colours, so if you have to use a lot to achieve a dark shade, it shouldn't make the icing too unmanageable and soggy. Most cake decoration shops stock a vast range of colours and you should also be able to find a limited range in the home baking section in some of the larger supermarkets. However, if you can only get hold of liquid colour, don't despair. It is possible to use it but you may have to knead a lot of icing sugar into the icing to stop it from becoming too wet.

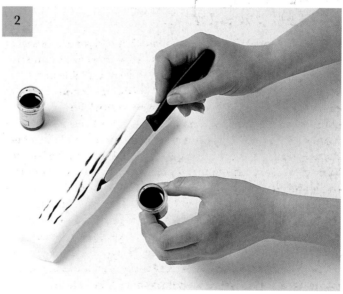

Apply the paste using the tip of a knife (2) or a cocktail stick. To achieve an unusual shade, you can use more than one colour at a time. If you are creating a new colour, keep a count of how many "dabs" of paste you use and which colours you apply so that you can replicate it later. Then, it's just a question of kneading it in. I am often asked how I get my colours looking so flat and even. The answer is simple – brute force! There is no alternative but to knead and knead and knead until the colour is evenly distributed.

Will the food colour stain?

Most of the colours will wash off your hands extremely easily but for protection against temporary staining from some of the more virulent shades, such as "sky blue" or "mint green", it is worth buying a pack of disposable polythene gloves from the supermarket. A clean pair of washing-up gloves kept especially for this use are an excellent alternative.

Can I mix sugarpaste (rolled fondant) with sugarpaste (rolled fondant)?

Yes, you can knead different coloured sugarpastes together to achieve an alternative colour or shade. For example, knead lumps of yellow and pink sugarpastes together to make a flesh colour, or black and white to make grey sugarpaste. If you make a colour that you might want to use again later, keep a note of the colours and rough quantities involved to make it easier to achieve a similar shade.

You can lighten a lump of coloured sugarpaste by kneading some white sugarpaste into it. Similarly, if you're trying to achieve a very dark colour, such as deep red or green, you can knead a little black sugarpaste into it. This will cut down on the amount of food colour you will need to use to create a dark tone. However, this little trick doesn't work with all colours. For example – kneading black sugarpaste into yellow will not give you a deep yellow, only an odd greyish concoction, so experiment with a small piece of sugarpaste first.

Creating special effects

Woodgrain effect

To achieve an easy woodgrain effect, first take a lump of white sugarpaste and a smaller lump of brown sugarpaste. Tear the brown icing into pieces and press it into the white. Roll the two colours together into a sausage, then bend it into a horseshoe shape. Roll the icing into a sausage again, and then fold and roll once more.

Continue until you see a woody effect starting to appear. If you roll the sugarpaste too much and the whole piece turns brown, re-roll some white sugarpaste back into it (3).

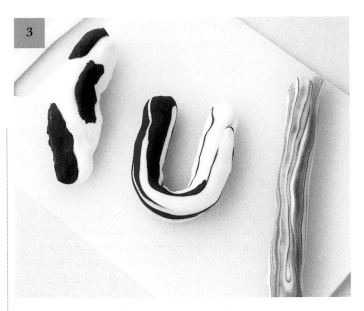

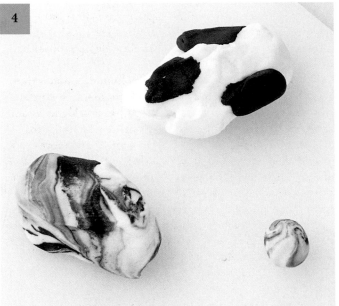

Marble effect

Again, this effective look is extremely easy to achieve. Take a lump of white sugarpaste and a smaller piece of the appropriate "vein" colour. In my case, I've used black and white for a white marble effect. Tear the smaller piece of sugarpaste into small pieces and press onto the white sugarpaste.

Carefully roll and knead the two colours together, as above for a woodgrain effect, until a marbled appearance begins to form. If you go too far, reknead a little white icing back into it. In the picture, I have pulled off a small piece and rolled it into a rounded shape for easy and effective pebble and rock shapes with which to decorate your cakes. These rocks also make extremely useful candleholders (4).

Multi-coloured effect

Break four or five different coloured lumps of sugarpaste into chunks and lightly press and roll together (if you roll it too much, it will turn into a brown colour). Then roll it out using a rolling pin and a flat, multi-coloured effect will appear (5).

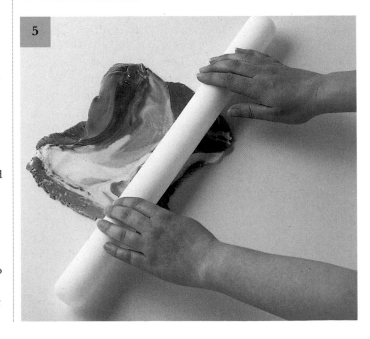

How do I stick the sugarpaste (rolled fondant) to the cake?

Sponge cakes

The best two "glues" I have found for sticking sugarpaste to the surface of a cake are buttercream (see recipe on page 19) and jam. Personally, I prefer buttercream but obviously it depends on the taste of the recipient. Once you have cut or carved the cake to shape, slice the cake horizontally into two pieces (or more if the cake is deep enough) and fill with buttercream or jam. One layer of each is a nice combination. Reassemble the cake and spread a thin layer of jam or buttercream over the sides and top using a palette knife. As you spread, any gaps or holes in the sponge should automatically be filled, providing a relatively smooth surface for the sugarpaste covering.

If your kitchen is especially hot and humid, you may find it worthwhile to put your buttercreamed cake into the fridge for a couple of hours to "set up". When you take it out again, it will feel like concrete at first but it will be a lot easier to cover as the layers will not be able to "squish" and move around. The refrigerated coated surface will have lost all its adhesive properties temporarily though, so before covering it with sugarpaste, spread another thin layer of buttercream over the top and sides of the cake.

In all of the cake projects, I have used buttercream to stick the sugarpaste to the cake – you can, of course, use jam as a substitute if you prefer.

Fruit cakes

If you are using a fruit cake, you will need to cover the cake with a layer of marzipan before the sugarpaste layer. This is to stop the oils from the fruit cake staining the sugarpaste.

To cover a cake with marzipan, first slice the top of the cake to make it level and turn it upside down on the cake board. If you wish, you can poke a few holes into the cake with a cocktail stick and drizzle a couple of tablespoons of rum or brandy over the top.

The marzipan is stuck to the cake using apricot jam because the taste doesn't interfere with that of the cake. It doesn't matter what brand you use – in fact, often a cheaper jam is better as it contains fewer lumps of fruit. Place a few tablespoons of the jam into a saucepan and heat gently to boiling point. Alternatively, microwave on full power for a couple of minutes until bubbling.

If there is a lot of fruit in your jam, pour it though a sieve to remove the lumps, making sure you press it through with a spoon. Take care as the jam is at boiling point. Then spread the jam over the top and sides of the cake using either a pastry brush or a palette knife. Dust your worksurface with icing sugar (never use cornflour as it can react with the

marzipan and cause fermentation), and roll out the marzipan. Lift and place over the cake. Smooth into position and trim the excess from the base.

To stick the sugarpaste to the marzipan, lightly brush the marzipan with either clear alcohol (such as gin or vodka), boiled water or, if you have some left over, the remaining boiled apricot jam. For instructions on covering cakes and cake boards with sugarpaste, see pages 21-22.

When I'm making models, how do I stick the pieces of sugarpaste (rolled fondant) together?

I have experimented with all sorts of sugar glues but the easiest, cheapest and least messy solution I have found is plain water. It will work perfectly well for the designs and figures in this book because all of the pieces are stuck together as soon as you make them, so the sugarpaste is still soft, malleable and slightly sticky. For sticking sugarpaste models together, I place cooled, boiled water from the kettle in a small jar kept solely for that purpose. However, if you find something else that works for you, then by all means stick with it (no pun intended).

The secret for successful and secure "sticking" is not to use too much liquid. If you use too much to stick an ear on the side of a character's head it will simply slide off. Again, if you haven't used enough water it will also fall off, so increase the amount. When you are modelling with sugarpaste, the icing should be pliable and is often fairly sticky. Therefore, it will usually take little more than a light dab of water and a gentle press with the tip of your finger to stick the pieces together, especially the very small elements, such as ears and hands (6).

Very occasionally there will be one element of a design that simply refuses to stay in place and needs sterner measures. The thing that gave me the most trouble in this book was the troll nestling amongst the fir trees on the Christmas cake – for some reason his nose refused to stay where it was put. It was finally fixed in place with a tiny dab of royal icing.

What should I use for cutting sugarpaste (rolled fondant)?

The best instrument for cutting shapes out of sugarpaste is a small, sharp, non-serrated knife (see Basic Equipment on page 28). When cutting the ends off a sausage shape or cutting out a thick square or rectangle, hold the knife as you

would when you're eating and slice normally. If you're cutting around a template or cutting out a thin, flat shape such as a leaf then hold the knife virtually upright and cut the sugarpaste using the tip of the knife (7).

If you have something very thin and intricate to cut out, then I would suggest using a scalpel with a 10A blade which you can buy from cake decoration and art shops.

How long can I store my sugarpaste (rolled fondant) models and will the colours fade?

Sugarpaste models can be made up to a month in advance of the date when you need them. Store them in a tin or cardboard box with a lid (never an airtight plastic container) and place in a cool place until required. Don't put them in a fridge or damp garage or they will go soggy. A lid of some sorts is important to protect them from dust and flies and, most important of all, sunlight, because bright daylight will cause the colours to fade.

After their public debut at the party, the birthday person may want to keep the models. The sugar in the icing acts as a preservative and there is nothing in them that will go mouldy, so your models can be kept indefinitely in a box. Out on a shelf, however, the colours will fade and they will become brittle in time and susceptible to moisture. (You can prolong their life slightly by varnishing them using a special varnish available from cake decorating shops.)

Troubleshooting

Cracks

Don't despair! This happens to all of us at times. It usually occurs because the sugarpaste has not been kneaded for long enough and therefore is not suitably warm and pliable for use. By far the easiest solution is to hide an offending crack with another model or decoration.

Usually, cracks or creases in chunky shapes, such as sausage or ball shapes, can be got rid of by simply rekneading and reshaping the sugarpaste. If you still have a hairline crack, then gently stroke it away using the pad of your finger. Do think ahead, though, perhaps the shape could be positioned so that the crack is hidden or facing the back of the cake.

Sometimes cracking happens because the sugarpaste is old or has already started to dry out. Microwaving can also cause problems (see page 8). Always cut off any crusty edges from microwaved sugarpaste before using and discard them.

If you have covered your cake with white sugarpaste, and found cracking on the edges, this can usually be hidden by dipping your finger in a little icing sugar and rubbing the sugarpaste gently in a circular motion to fill the cracks. For coloured sugarpastes, take a small lump of the same coloured sugarpaste and polish its base on a shiny surface, then rub the polished surface over the cracks, again using a circular motion.

An alternative method is the plasterer technique. Colour a little royal icing to the same shade as the cake. Spread over the cracks, then carefully scrape away the excess with a knife. This should leave the fractures both filled and hidden.

Watermarks

The secret behind getting rid of watermarks is to deal with them as soon as they occur. If you accidentally splash or drip water onto your cake, wipe it away immediately. If you leave it for too long, the drip will start to dissolve the surface of the sugarpaste and you'll be left with an unsightly hollow. If the sugarpaste is still soft you may be able to smooth out the problem by rubbing gently, in a circular motion, with the tip of your finger. Be careful, though, or you could cause the sugarpaste around the watermark to fracture and crack causing an even bigger problem than before. If all else fails and you're left with an unsightly blemish in an obvious place, resort to the "tried and trusted, never failed yet" technique of placing something over the top!

Air bubbles under the sugarpaste (rolled fondant)

These occur when air gets trapped underneath the sugarpaste as you cover the cake.

Once you have rolled out and lifted the sugarpaste onto the cake, it is important to start smoothing it into position from the top first. That way, any air on the top of the cake will be expelled out and under the sides before you press these into position.

It is also important to make sure that the buttercream or jam covering the sponge is still tacky. If it has dried out, it won't hold the sugarpaste in position. If some time has passed since you covered your cake, touch and check that it still feels sticky. If it doesn't, spread another thin layer over the cake.

Another tip is not to roll your sugarpaste too thin when covering the cake. A covering less than 5 mm (1/8 in) thick is more prone to air bubbles.

If, despite all your care, you still find an offending lump – resort to more drastic measures. Holding a clean dressmaker's pin or a cocktail stick at an angle, poke a small hole into the bubble and gently press out the air.

Icing sugar marks

These can be removed after the cake is assembled. First of all, gently brush over your masterpiece with a soft brush, such as a pastry brush (use a smaller paintbrush over delicate areas or models). That should remove most of the "dust". For more stubborn areas, wipe away marks using a damp (not wet) paintbrush or a soft, lightly moistened, clean cloth.

Don't worry about how it looks initially, the shiny damp areas will revert to a matt finish in a few hours, depending on the temperature and humidity in your room.

Frayed edges when cutting sugarpaste

To cut sugarpaste cleanly, you need a small, sharp, non-serrated knife. A scalpel (available from stationery shops) is also useful for trimming edges and making intricate cuts.

When I turn my cake over to get a nice flat surface on the top, I get a large gap between the base of the cake and the board

If the cake is very rounded, slice away some of the cake before turning it over. If you are using sponge cake and the gap is not too large, simply fill it with buttercream as you coat the outside. If it is too large to do this, roll out a sugarpaste "sausage". Flatten one edge with your finger and slide into the gap (8). Trim away the excess with a sharp knife.

The same procedure is also used on fruitcakes using marzipan instead of sugarpaste.

Basic Recipes

I really believe that it is important for a cake to taste as good as it looks. To help you achieve success in the taste test area, here is a collection of tried and trusted recipes for all the cakes and icings that you might need. There's even a luxurious truffle recipe to help you use up all the leftover bits of cake, because you won't want to throw them away!*

Madeira sponge cake

This recipe is probably the quickest, easiest and tastiest sponge cake recipe that you'll ever come across. You simply throw everything in the bowl together, mix and bake. It produces a firm moist cake that is excellent for carving into shapes. It will freeze for up to three months. (C = cup/st = stick)

Method

1 Grease and line the relevant cake tin and pre-heat the oven to 150ºC/300ºF/Gas 2.

2 Sift the flour into a mixing bowl and add all the other ingredients. Bind them together carefully using a slow speed setting on your mixer (to stop flour from flying everywhere) then increase the speed and beat for one minute.

3 Spoon the mixture into the prepared tin and smooth the top. Bake in the centre of the oven. Test the cake at the end of the cooking time. If you can hear a lot of bubbling and it still looks very pale leave it in for another quarter of an hour. Test again later by inserting a knife or skewer. If it comes out clean, the cake is cooked. Leave in the tin for five minutes, then turn out onto a wire rack to cool.

Square tin		15 cm (6 in)	18 cm (7 in)	20 cm (8 in)
Round tin	15 cm (6 in)	18 cm (7 in)	20 cm (8 in)	23 cm (9 in)
Self-raising flour	170 g (6 oz/1¼ C)	230 g (8 oz/2 C)	285 g (10 oz/2½ C)	350 g (12 oz/3 C)
Caster (superfine) sugar	115 g (4 oz/½ C)	170 g (6 oz/¾ C)	230 g (8 oz/1 C)	285 g (10 oz/1¼ C)
Butter (softened)	115 g (4 oz/1 st)	170 g (6 oz/1½ st)	230 g (8 oz/2 st)	285 g (10 oz/2½ st)
Eggs (medium)	2	3	4	5
Milk	1 tbsp	1½ tbsp	2 tbsp	2 tbsp
Baking time (approx.)	1¼ hrs	1½ – 2 hrs	1¾ – 2 hrs	2 – 2¼ hrs

Taste variations

It's easy to vary the cake's flavour. To add a touch of citrus, mix the grated zest of an orange or lemon to the mixture before cooking. Alternatively a teaspoon of almond essence or 30 g (1 oz/¼ cup) desiccated (shredded) coconut turns an ordinary Madeira into something quite exotic!

Colour variations

Food colours needn't be limited to use on the outside of the cake. Swirling a little food colour into the mixture before cooking will result in a marbled sponge. Alternatively you could mix it in more thoroughly for a solid coloured sponge.

Fairy cakes

To make the little fairy cakes for the Caterpillar cake, simply mix up the recipe amount required for a 15 cm (6 in) square Madeira sponge cake. Divide into portions and mix a different food colour paste into each portion (apply slowly with a knife). Then spoon into paper cake cases and bake in the middle of the oven (180ºC/350ºF/Gas 4) for about 15 minutes. This should make about 15 cakes.

Pudding bowl & loaf tin cakes

If you are baking a cake in a 1 litre pudding bowl or 900 g (2 lb) loaf tin for cakes such as the Wicked Witch or Racing Car, again use the recipe amounts for the 15 cm (6 in) square cake.

To prepare a heatproof pudding bowl, grease the inside and place a disc of greaseproof paper or baking parchment at the base of the bowl. When cooked (and because it is so thick, this could take up to 2 hours), slide a knife around the outside of the bowl and tip the cake out onto a rack.

Do the same with the loaf tin. Grease the insides and lay a strip of greaseproof (waxed) along the bottom. Slide a knife down the sides of the cake to loosen after cooking and turn out as before.

Chocolate chip cake

To make a chocolate chip pudding bowl cake, as used for the chocolate Rag Doll cake, make up the mixture as for the 15 cm (6 in) square cake as described above and stir in 100 g (3½ oz) chocolate chips. Spoon the mixture into the prepared bowl and bake for the appropriate amount of time.

Chocolate sponge cake

This wonderful recipe produces a cake with a velvety soft texture. Always try to use good strong plain chocolate when making this cake. A crust will form on the top when cooking which may even scorch slightly – this is perfectly normal. All the crust should be cut off and discarded before decorating. This cake will freeze for up to three months. (C = cup/st = stick)

Method

1 Pre-heat the oven to 180ºC/350ºF/Gas 4. Grease and line the tin and separate the eggs.
2 Melt the chocolate, either in a small bowl suspended over a pan of simmering water or in a heatproof bowl in the microwave. Do not get any water into the chocolate.
3 Cream the butter and caster sugar together.
4 Beat in the egg yolks and then the melted chocolate.
5 Set the mixer to a slow speed and add the flour. Mix very lightly, just until all the flour is incorporated.
6 Scrape the chocolate mixture into a spare bowl and wash and dry the mixing bowl (you must get rid of any grease).
7 Attach the whisk attachment to your mixer and whisk the egg whites into stiff peaks. Whisk in the sifted icing sugar.
8 Reattach the beater to the mixer and slowly mix the chocolate mixture into the egg whites. Pour into the prepared tin and bake immediately.
9 Because of the crust, it is sometimes difficult to tell if the cake is cooked. If there is a very strong smell of chocolate in your kitchen then that's a good sign. Cut away a piece of crust and insert a knife or skewer. If it comes out clean, the cake should be cooked. Leave in tin for five minutes, then turn out.

Square tin		15 cm (6 in)	18 cm (7 in)	20 cm (8 in)
Round tin	15 cm (6 in)	18 cm (7 in)	20 cm (8 in)	23 cm (9 in)
Eggs (medium)	3	4	6	8
Plain chocolate	150 g (5 oz)	170 g (6 oz)	230 g (8 oz)	285 g (10 oz)
Butter	90 g (3 oz/¾ st)	120 g (4 oz/1 st)	170 g (6 oz/1½ st)	230 g (8 oz/2 st)
Caster (superfine) sugar	45 g (1 ½ oz/¼ C)	75 g (2 ½ oz/⅓ C)	120 g (4 oz/½ C)	150 g (5 oz/¾ C)
Self-raising flour	90 g (3 oz/⅔ C)	120 g (4 oz/1 C)	170 g (6 oz/1½ C)	230 g (8 oz/2⅔C)
Icing (confectioners') sugar	30 g (1 oz/¼ C)	30 g (1 oz/¼ C)	60 g (2 oz/⅓ C)	90 g (3 oz/½C)
Baking time (approx.)	40–55 mins	45 mins –1 hr	1–1¼ hrs	1 – 1½ hrs

Fruit cakes

As well as a recipe for a traditional rich fruit cake oozing with nuts and brandy-soaked fruit, I have also included two non-alcoholic fruit cakes, both of which are slightly sweeter and will perhaps appeal more to children.

Although many people think that making a fruit cake must be a huge binding chore, it's really not. Once you have got all the ingredients together you literally just throw them in, mix them round and bake. You also get the added bonus of being able to make a wish as you stir the mixture and a wonderful aroma floating through your home. You can't buy that at the supermarket!

The amounts given here are for a 20 cm (8 in) round cake. Although not absolutely essential, the rich fruit cake will benefit from being made up to three months in advance and being "fed" every couple of weeks with a little brandy (just drizzle it over the top of the cake and reseal). However, the other two cakes can be made and iced straightaway.

Preparing the tin

Because fruit cakes take so long to cook, it is really worth the effort of double lining the tin to protect the outside of the cake as it cooks. I prefer to use greaseproof paper for this but baking parchment will work just as well.

Rub a little butter or margarine around the inside of the tin to grease it. Cut a sheet of greaseproof paper off the roll long enough to go right around the tin. Cut it in half lengthways to make two long strips. Fold the two strips in half along the length. Place one strip inside the tin to line it and the other around the outside. Tie string round the outside of the tin to hold the external wrapping in place.

Using the baking tin itself as a template, draw around it on another piece of greaseproof paper. Place a second piece underneath the first sheet and cut out two circles of greaseproof paper at the same time, cutting just inside the line. Place these on the base of the tin.

Traditional rich fruit cake

Ingredients

175 g (6 oz / 1 heaped cup) currants
175 g (6 oz / 1 heaped cup) raisins
175 g (6 oz / 1 heaped cup) sultanas
40 g (1½ oz / 3 tbsp) mixed peel
75 g (2½ oz / ½ cup) glacé (candied) cherries (halved)
90 ml (6 tbsp) brandy (for drizzling)
175 g (6 oz / 1½ sticks) butter
175 g (6 oz / 1 heaped cup) soft dark brown sugar
4 medium eggs
200 g (7 oz / 1¾ cups) plain (all-purpose) flour
1 tsp mixed (pumpkin-pie) spice
½ tsp cinnamon
30 g (1 oz) ground almonds
Grated zest of 1 lemon
30 g (1 oz) flaked almonds

Method

1 If you have time, place all the dried fruits into a mixing bowl with the brandy. Stir and cover and leave for a few hours, preferably overnight.
2 Grease and double line the cake tin as described above and pre-heat the oven to 150°C/300°F/Gas 2.
3 Cream the butter and sugar together, then beat in the eggs. Gently stir in the sifted flour, spices and ground almonds (add a little more flour if the mixture is at all runny).
4 Stir in the soaked dried fruits, lemon zest and flaked almonds.
5 Spoon into the prepared tin. Level the top and bake for 2¾ hours. To check whether the cake is ready, insert a skewer or a small sharp, non-serrated knife into the centre. If it comes out clean, the cake is ready. If not, bake for another 15 minutes.
Leave the cake to cool in the tin.

Storing the cake

To store after cooling, pierce the top of the cake a few times with a cocktail stick. Drizzle with a little brandy and double wrap the cake in greaseproof paper. Then double wrap in two sheets of aluminium foil and place in a tin or cool cupboard. Never store in an airtight plastic container. "Feed" by drizzling with a little brandy about once a week. The cake should keep for about three months.

Chocolate fruit cake

This is one of those recipes which at first glance you think couldn't possibly work. Well it does – brilliantly!

Ingredients

175 g (6 oz / 1½ sticks) butter
175 g (6 oz / ¾ cup) brown sugar
4 medium eggs
115 g (4 oz / 1 cup) plain (all-purpose) flour
115 g (4 oz / 1 cup) self-raising flour
15 g (½ oz / 2½ tbsp) cocoa (unsweetened cocoa)
100 g (3½ oz / ¾ cup) currants
100 g (3½ oz / ¾ cup) raisins
100 g (3½ oz / ¾ cup) sultanas
75 g (2½ oz / ½ cup) glacé (candied) cherries (halved)
100 g (3½ oz) milk chocolate drops
15 ml (1 tbsp) rum flavouring

Method

1 Line and prepare a 20 cm (8 in) round tin as described above and pre-heat the oven to 150°C/300°F/Gas 2.
2 Cream the butter and sugar together, then beat in the eggs.
3 Sift the flours and cocoa together and stir into the mixture.
4 Stir in the fruit, the chocolate drops and the rum flavouring.
5 Spoon into the prepared tin and bake in the middle of the oven for about 1½ – 2 hours. Leave to cool in the tin before turning out. Store as above.

Tropical fruit cake

The secret ingredient in this little gem of a cake is pineapple. If you wish, you can soak the dried fruit overnight in rum and drizzle a couple of tablespoons over the cooked cake before decorating but it works just as well without alcohol.

Ingredients

200 g (7 oz / 1⅛ cups) self raising flour
½ tsp mixed (pumpkin-pie) spice
½ tsp cinnamon
225 g (8 oz) crushed tinned pineapple (well-drained)
150 g (5 oz / 1 ¼ sticks) butter
125 g (4½ oz / ⅔ cup) soft brown sugar
2 large eggs
30 ml (2 tbsp) milk
75 g (2½ oz / ½ cup) glacé (candied) cherries (halved)
120 g (4 oz / 1 cup) sultanas
120 g (4 oz / 1 cup) raisins
120 g (4 oz / 1 cup) currants

Method

1 Line and prepare a 20 cm (8 in) round tin as described above and pre-heat the oven to 170°C/325°F/Gas 3.
2 Sift the flour and spices together into a bowl.
3 Tip the pineapple into the now empty sieve and allow to drain well.
4 Cream the butter and sugar together, then beat in the eggs.
5 Fold in the flour and milk.
6 Roll the cherries in a little flour and add to the mixture. Sir in the fruit and the pineapple.
7 Bake in the centre of the oven for about 1½ hours. Leave to cool in the tin before turning out. Store as above.

Microwave cakes

These may not have exactly the same texture or appearance as the real thing but the advantage is that they only take four minutes to cook. They look a lot paler than a cake cooked in a traditional oven but after they've been covered with lashings of buttercream, they'll disappear in a very traditional manner!

The amounts given are for an 18 cm (7 in) round microwave cake pan or a 1 litre heatproof pudding bowl. Never use a metal cake tin in a microwave.

Microwave vanilla cake

120 g (4 oz / 1 stick) butter
120 g (4 oz / ½ cup) caster (superfine) sugar
2 large eggs
1 tsp vanilla essence
120 g (4 oz / 1 cup) self-raising flour
½ tsp baking powder

Method

1 Grease and place a greaseproof paper disc on the base of the cake pan or bowl.
2 Cream the butter and sugar together.
3 Beat in the eggs and vanilla essence.
4 Stir in the flour and baking powder.
5 Spoon the mixture into the prepared pan and cook on full power for 4 minutes. Stand for ten minutes before turning out.

Microwave chocolate cake

120 g (4 oz / 1 stick) butter
120 g (4 oz / ½ cup) caster (superfine) sugar
2 large eggs
30 g (1 oz / 5 tbsp) cocoa powder (unsweetened cocoa)
90 g (3 oz / ¾ cup) self-raising flour
1 tsp baking powder

Method

1 Follow steps 1-3 as for the vanilla cake above (omitting the vanilla essence in step 3).
2 Stir in the cocoa, flour and baking powder.
3 Cook on full power for four minutes. Leave to stand for ten minutes before turning out.

Gingerbread

90 g (3 oz / ¾ stick) butter
150 g (5 oz / ¾ cup) soft brown sugar
90 g (3 oz / ⅛ cup) golden (corn) syrup
425 g (15 oz / 3 cups) plain (all-purpose) flour (plus about 30 g/1 oz/3 tbsp) for rolling out)
1 tsp baking powder
2 tsp ground ginger
1 tsp mixed (pumpkin-pie) spice
1 medium egg (beaten)
Currants and glacé (candied) cherries (optional)

Method

1 Gently heat the butter, sugar and syrup until the sugar has dissolved. Leave to cool slightly for about five minutes.
2 Pre-heat the oven to 180°C/350°F/Gas 4 and lightly grease a couple of baking trays.
3 Sift the flour, baking powder and spices together into a mixing bowl and make a well in the centre.
4 Tip the melted mixture and the beaten egg into the centre. First bind the mixture together using a knife, then use your hands to form a soft dough.
5 Sprinkle your worksurface with flour and roll out the gingerbread to about 3 mm (⅛ in) thick.
6 Cut out the figures using cutters and trace around the house template (see page 142) using a sharp knife. Re-knead and re-roll the gingerbread as necessary.
7 Lift using a fish slice or palette knife and place onto the baking tray. If you wish to use currants and cherries for eyes, mouth and buttons, gently press these into the gingerbread at this stage. Bake for about 15 minutes in the centre of the oven.
8 Transfer the cooked gingerbread to a cooling rack and decorate in whatever manner you wish when cold.

Chocolate truffles

These are an extremely easy and delicious way of using up leftover bits of cake (vanilla, chocolate or fruit). The trouble is that they are so delicious, you may find yourself having to cook a spare cake especially for the truffles! Boxed up they would make lovely presents.

To make, use approximately 30 g (1 oz) chocolate for every 30 g (1 oz) of cake crumbs.

Melt the chocolate in a heatproof bowl and stir in the crumbs. Roll into ball shapes and either place in tiny paper cases or arrange on a plate. Decorate with melted chocolate

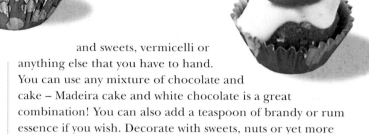

and sweets, vermicelli or anything else that you have to hand.

You can use any mixture of chocolate and cake – Madeira cake and white chocolate is a great combination! You can also add a teaspoon of brandy or rum essence if you wish. Decorate with sweets, nuts or yet more chocolate. Experiment and have fun!

Icing Recipes

Buttercream

Buttercream is wonderfully versatile for filling and decorating cakes, as it can be coloured, stippled or piped. This recipe makes up one quantity as referred to in the cake designs. If you have a lot left over, you can freeze it for up to one month.

250 g (8 oz / 2 sticks) butter
450 g (1 lb / 3¼ cups) icing (confectioners') sugar
1 tbsp hot water
1 tsp vanilla essence

Method
1 Beat the butter until soft and fluffy.
2 Mix in the sugar, water and essence and beat until soft.

Taste variations

For chocolate buttercream, either mix in 100 g (3½ oz) melted white or plain chocolate or 1 tbsp cocoa powder (unsweetened cocoa) mixed to a paste with 1–2 tbsp hot water.

For coffee flavouring, mix 1 tbsp instant coffee into 1 tbsp water and beat into the buttercream.

Alternatively you can substitute peppermint, lemon or almond essence in place of vanilla to vary the taste.

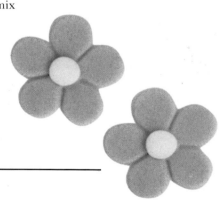

Sugarpaste (rolled fondant)

Although ready-made sugarpaste is easily available, here is a home-made version that works just as well.

Treat it as you would a commercial brand but use within one week of preparation.

500 g (1 lb 2 oz / 3¼ cups) icing (confectioners') sugar
1 egg white (or equivalent amount of dried egg white mixed with water)
30 ml (2 tbsp) liquid glucose (available from chemists, supermarkets and cake decorating equipment shops)

Method
1 Place the icing sugar into a bowl and make a well in the centre.
2 Tip the egg white and glucose into the well and stir in using a wooden spoon.
3 Finish binding the icing together with your hands, kneading until all the sugar is incorporated and the icing feels silky and smooth.
4 Double wrap immediately in two small plastic bags. It may be used straightaway.

Royal icing

Traditionally, royal icing is made with real egg white. However, because of the slight possibility of salmonella poisoning, it is better to use dried egg white instead. This works just as well and is easily available from supermarkets.

Read the instructions on the packet in case they differ slightly from the ones I've given here.

20 g (¾ oz) dried egg white
90 ml (2½ fl oz / ⅓ cup) cold water
500 g (1 lb 2 oz / 3¼ cups) icing (confectioners') sugar

Method

1 Mix the egg white and water in a bowl until smooth.
2 Sieve the icing sugar into a grease-free bowl.
3 Tip in the egg mixture and beat on the slowest speed for five minutes until the icing stands up in peaks.
4 Place the icing into a airtight plastic bowl with a lid. Lay a piece of cling film directly on top of the icing and replace the lid. Always keep covered when not in use.

Gelatin icing

60 ml (4 tbsp) water
1 sachet (approx 12 g / 1 oz) gelatin powder
10 ml (2 tsp) liquid glucose
500 g (1 lb 2 oz / 41/2 cups) icing (confectioners') sugar
1–4 tbsp cornflour (cornstarch)

Method

1 Place the water in a bowl and sprinkle over the gelatin powder. Leave for 2 minutes. Heat the mixture over a pan of boiling water until the gelatin dissolves.
2 Remove from the heat and stir in the glucose. Allow to cool for a minute.
3 Sieve the icing sugar into a bowl, make a well in the centre and stir in the gelatin mixture. When it has bound together knead it to a dough, adding cornflour as required.

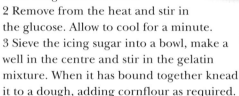

Colouring desiccated (shredded) coconut and sugar granules

This is probably the quickest way of all to cover a cake board. If dessicated coconut is coloured green, it makes realistic looking grass. If coloured grey or brown, it makes marvellous gravel.

Place the coconut into a small bowl and add a small amount of food colour paste. Mix in the colour slowly, adding more as necessary. It is easiest to do this using your hand. (Wear a disposable plastic glove for protection to prevent your hands from staining.)

You can also colour sugar granules in the same way but beware, it does make for a rather crunchy cake!

Basic Techniques

Covering cakes with sugarpaste (rolled fondant)

Round cakes

To cover a round cake, either shop-bought or home-made, first make sure that your sugarpaste is well-kneaded and pliable. Measure the height and diameter of your cake. Double the height and add this measurement to the diameter, making a note of the total.

Dust your worksurface and rolling pin with icing sugar and roll out the sugarpaste to the size you've just calculated. Don't roll the sugarpaste to any less than 5 mm (⅛ in) thick (if this means that the sugarpaste has to be slightly less wide than your measurement, it shouldn't matter as it will stretch once it is in position).

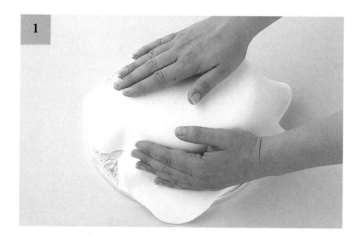

To transfer the sugarpaste from your worksurface onto the cake, you can roll it around your rolling pin and, holding it over the far edge of the cake, pull the rolling pin back towards you allowing the icing to fall and drape over the top of the cake. Alternatively, slide your hands flat, palms upwards under the sugarpaste, and lift and place the icing on top of the cake. If the sugarpaste appears to be sticking to your worksurface, slide a long palette knife underneath it to loosen.

To smooth the rolled sugarpaste into position, start from the top of the cake. Gently stroke the icing away from the centre of the cake to dispel any air trapped between the icing and the cake. Smooth it with the flat of your hand (1) then slide your hands over and around the sides. If the sugarpaste doesn't quite reach the cake board, ease it down by pressing and gently pushing with the side of your hand.

For a final finishing touch, gently rub the heel of your hand over the sugarpaste using a soft, circular motion as though you were gently polishing it. You can also run over the surface with a cake smoother for a really professional touch.

Square cakes

It is just as easy to cover a square cake with sugarpaste as a round cake. The secret is to make sure that you have rolled out the sugarpaste so that it is wide enough to cover the cake comfortably. If you have to pull and stretch the sugarpaste too much it is likely to catch and tear on the corners.

Measure the height, double it and add to the width of your cake. Roll the sugarpaste out to the measurement calculated, and lift and place on top of the cake (as described above). Again, start by smoothing out the icing on the top of the cake using the flat of your hand. Then move on to the sides. Start with a downward stroke with your palm flat against the sides of the cake so that the edge of your hand pushes the icing gently down towards the board. If it starts to form a pleat, hook a finger underneath the icing and pull gently to fan the icing out. Then carefully press the icing into position. Trim away any excess icing from around the base.

The corners and edges on a square or rectangular sugarpasted cake will always be softly rounded so do not spend anxious, frustrating minutes trying to create a razor sharp crease.

Covering cake boards

The all-in-one method

This is by far the easiest and quickest way of covering a board. You do it before the cake is placed onto the board to avoid the need to trim and fit sugarpaste around the cake.

Lightly moisten the cake board with a little water and place it to one side. Knead the sugarpaste until it is pliable and begin to roll it out on your worksurface. Before it has reached the size of the board, lift and place it onto the board. Continue to roll the icing up to and over the edges of the board (2). Smooth it into position with either the flat of your hand or a cake smoother, then trim away the excess and neaten the edges.

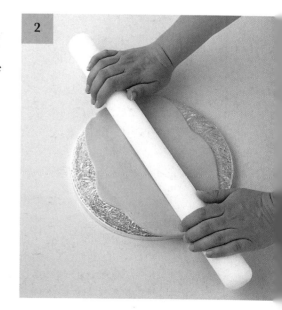

Some people prefer to cut out the icing in the middle, where the cake will eventually sit, at this stage. This is because, after a couple of days, the moisture in

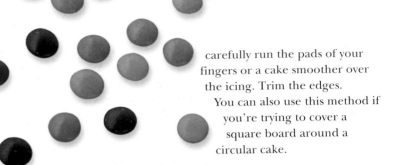

the cake will start to dissolve the sugarpaste on the board beneath it. However, in my experience, the cakes are usually eaten so fast that there's little time for any real damage to be done and so far, nobody's ever complained to me about a soggy bottom!

The bandage method

This method of covering the cake board is used after the cake itself is covered and in position on the board. It works best for round, oblong or slightly irregular-shaped cakes.

Run a tape measure around the sides of the cake and make a note of the measurement. Ensure that your worksurface is well dusted with icing sugar and roll some sugarpaste into a thin strip which is slightly longer than the circumference of the cake (as measured) and slightly wider than the exposed cake board (the distance between the side of the cake and the edge of the board). Slice a little icing off one of the long sides of the strip to create a neat edge (the remaining icing should still be slightly wider than the exposed cake board). Moisten the board with a little water. Slide a knife under and along the strip to loosen any sections that might be stuck to the worksurface and roll the sugarpaste up like a loose bandage.

Starting from the back of the cake, slowly unwind the "bandage" over the board so that the cut edge of the strip lies flush against the base of the cake (3). Neaten the join and

carefully run the pads of your fingers or a cake smoother over the icing. Trim the edges.

You can also use this method if you're trying to cover a square board around a circular cake.

Covering the board around a square cake

Apart from the all-in-one method, this is the easiest way to cover either a round or square cake board surrounding a square cake.

Roll out the sugarpaste to a thickness of about 3 mm (⅛ in) and cut out four strips slightly longer and slightly wider than the sides of the exposed cake board. Moisten the cake board with a little water and lay one strip along each side so that they overlap at the ends (4). Make a diagonal cut from the edge of the board to the edge of the cake at each corner and remove the excess icing pieces at each corner. You should now be left with a neat mitred join at all four corners. Smooth the icing and run a sharp knife around the edges to trim away the excess.

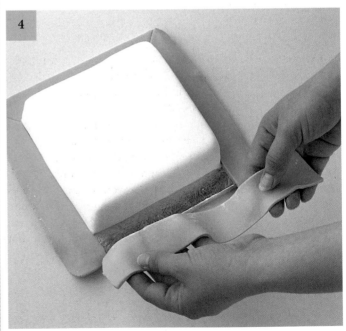

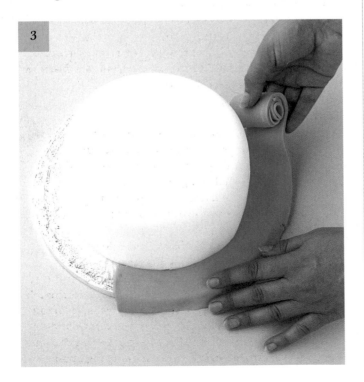

This technique of covering the board in sections also works if you're trying to cover the board around an irregular shape such as the Racing Car on page 70. Moisten the board with water and roll out your sugarpaste. Cut it into sections and lay around the cake until the board is covered. Make a cut across any overlapping icing and lift and remove the excess. Run a knife around the edges to neaten them.

Ribbons on boards

Apart from the Space Age cake (page 90), if you look at any of the main cake photos in the book, you will see that each one is finished off with a ribbon around the edge of the cake board. This little touch is by no means obligatory. It is always done in competitions and displays in the sugarcraft world and it's a habit I just can't seem to kick!

If you'd like to do the same to your cakes, measure the circumference of the board and cut a piece of ribbon to just over that length (allow roughly 10 mm (⅜ in) extra for the overlap). The height of a cake board in this country is usually 12 mm (½ in) but most haberdashers only stock ribbons at widths of 15 mm (⅝ in). Your local cake decorating shop should have a stock of 12 mm width ribbon in various colours.

The best method I have found for keeping the ribbon in place is by using short lengths of double-sided tape. Other methods are non-toxic glue, dressmaking pins or dabs of royal icing. Glue and royal icing may bleed through and discolour the ribbon, and I would never recommend pins on any cake, especially one designed for a child for obvious reasons.

Modelling with sugarpaste (rolled fondant)

Making figures

If you pull one of the figures in this book apart you will find that in fact it is made out of very simple and easy-to-make shapes. Heads are usually ball shaped, torsos slightly oval and legs are long and sausage-like (5).

When making figures, you have to take into account various factors such as gravity and the strength and ability of the medium itself. Sugarpaste is not ideal for making a three-dimensional ballerina standing on one leg – it simply cannot dry hard or strong enough. That is why you will find that most of the characters in this book are either sitting, lying or using the sides of the cake as support. If your character still seems a little wobbly, then resort to some secret support. Insert a short strand of raw, dried spaghetti or a candy stick. Try to avoid using cocktail sticks as these could cause injury to the unwary eater.

It is for these reasons that bed and settee cakes are extremely valuable designs to master. Once you can make a bed, you can put anything or anyone in it from Father Christmas to the family dog!

All the figures in this book are stuck together using water. The secret is not to use too much or bits will fall off! If you haven't already done so, read through the "Introduction to Sugarpaste" section (see pages 8–13) which deals with colouring and using sugarpaste in more detail.

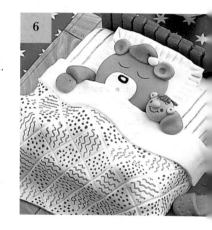

Dressing your characters is the way to really bring them to life. If you are making a cake for somebody who always wears a suit or a certain shirt, dress the character on the cake likewise for added humour. Patterns can be painted on with food colour (6) and small details such as collars or buttons can be cut or rolled out of sugarpaste. Another extremely quick and easy way to make buttons is to press small circles down the front of a character's tummy with the end of a drinking straw.

Making faces

It's amazingly easy to create a variety of different expressions without the need for any artistic skills. Can you draw an exclamation mark? A simple line and dot? Because if so, you can also draw a whole range of different faces.

Over the page are ten drawn examples of very simple faces pulling ten very different expressions and they are all done using just dots and lines (7).

I recommend that you use black food colour and a fine paintbrush to paint the faces onto the sugarpaste. (See "Painting on sugarpaste" on page 26 for further tips.) Alternatively, you could use a food colour pen (a type of felt tip pen that uses food colour instead of ink) which you can buy in cake decorating shops. However, you must allow the sugarpaste to harden for a few hours first otherwise the nib of the pen will rip and tear the surface of the sugarpaste.

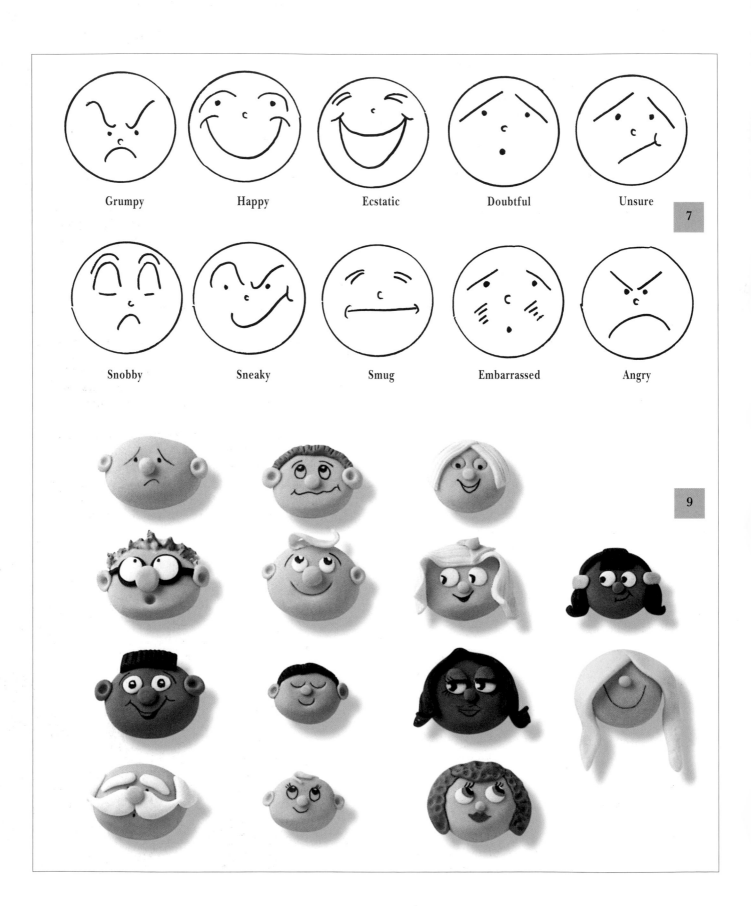

Grumpy   Happy   Ecstatic   Doubtful   Unsure

7

Snobby   Sneaky   Smug   Embarrassed   Angry

9

24

A beautiful female face is slightly more difficult but only because you have to try to paint on eyelashes as fine as possible (8). If they're too thick, she'll look like a drag queen!

Alternatively, features such as eyes can be made out of small balls of sugarpaste. Hair can be piped or smeared on using royal icing or buttercream. It can also be cut out of sugarpaste and styled in a multitude of fashions to suit the character of the cake or the recipient (9). You can even press sugarpaste through something such as a sieve or garlic press (washed of course!) to make the most amazing dreadlocks.

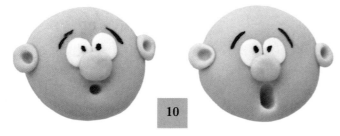

It is useful to note that on most people – ears tend to be level with the eyes. Also, for some reason, my men tend to have bigger noses than my women!

Never underestimate the power of the end of a humble paintbrush! Poke a hollow with it to make an "oh!" expression. Poke and pull it downwards and your character immediately starts singing his heart out (10).

You can also make expressions just by poking curved objects such as icing nozzles or drinking straws into the sugarpaste while it's still soft (11).

When it comes to skin tones, the best colour I have found for white tones is a shade of food colour paste called "paprika", available from cake decoration equipment shops. Alternatively, you can knead a little pink, yellow and white sugarpaste together. For darker skins, use "dark brown" or "chestnut" food colour pastes (11).

Making animals

Many of the same rules apply to making animals out of sugarpaste. Pull a model apart and you'll see that again the basic components are easy-to-make shapes (12). In fact, once you can master the cone, sausage and ball, you can immediately make a teddy, rabbit and baby (13). Baby? Okay so perhaps baby shouldn't come under the animal heading but it's another demonstration of how incredibly versatile these basic shapes can be.

Remember that the finished cake will probably be picked up and moved around. It might even have to travel long distances in a car, so make sure that the models have nice chunky bottoms to sit on, so that they don't fall over and that any appendages – trunks, arms, legs, ears, etc – are stuck down securely, without challenging the laws of gravity.

If you are planning to make a whole cake in the shape of an animal, it might be worth making a small sugarpaste prototype first. This way you can experiment with colours and proportions without fear of too much wastage. You might also come across new ideas to improve the design along the way.

Sugarpaste models can be made at least one month in advance. Store them in a tin or cardboard box for protection (but not an airtight plastic container). Keep somewhere cool, such as a cupboard, but don't store somewhere damp such as the fridge or garage.

Painting on sugarpaste (rolled fondant)

This is another technique which can look extremely daunting. What if it goes wrong? Will the whole cake be ruined? Again, follow some simple rules and understand the medium and you should be painting masterpieces in no time.

Always use food colour to paint on cakes. You will find a vast range of paste colours in cake decoration equipment shops but you can start with just a few basics and mix them together as you would watercolour paints to get all sorts of colours and shades.

If possible, leave your sugarpasted cake overnight before painting. This means that the surface will have hardened and will be much easier to paint on. You are also less likely to dent the cake if you lean on it.

Brush the surface of the cake with a dry brush to remove any icing sugar which could cause colours to bleed. Place a few dabs of food colour onto a saucer and mix in a little water. You are now ready to start painting.

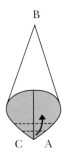

Paint a very light outline on the cake first or make yourself a template to transfer an image to the top of the cake. If you are planning to draw an outline around the image, paint the colour on before the black outline to stop the black from bleeding.

Correcting painted mistakes

To remove a painted mistake, dip a paintbrush into clean water and gently rub the area in a circular motion to break the colour up. Then wipe away with a clean, damp cloth. Leave to dry before repainting.

Piping techniques

Piping is another technique that tends to frighten people, but basic piping techniques are actually quite simple. Practise first on a spare board or worksurface if you don't believe me!

To make life easier, some supermarkets sell ready-made icing in tubes – just screw a nozzle on the end and pipe!

Cake decoration equipment and some kitchenware shops also sell ready-made piping bags but it's not that difficult to make your own.

Making a piping (decorating) bag

1 Cut some greaseproof (waxed) paper into a triangle.

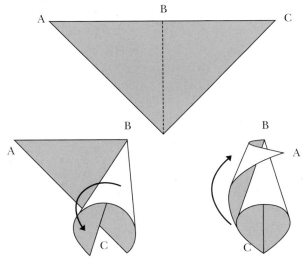

2 Pick up corner "C" and fold over, so that "B" forms a sharp cone in the centre.

3 Wrap corner "A" around the cone.

4 Make sure that "A" and "C" are at the back and that the point of the cone is sharp.

5 Fold points "A" and "C" inside the top edge of the bag to hold it securely. Snip off the end and insert a piping nozzle.

Piping

Place some icing into the bag and fold the end over a couple of times to seal it and force the icing down out of the nozzle.

To pipe around the base of a cake or the edge of something on a decorated background of a cake, a style of piping known as a "snail trail" is often used.

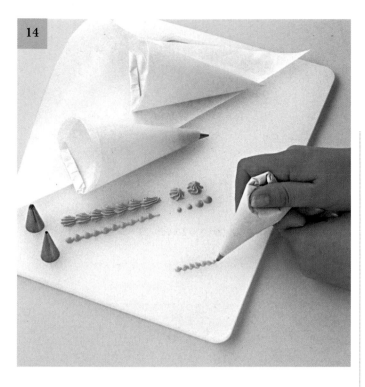

To do this you simply squeeze a little icing out of the nozzle, then keeping the tip of the nozzle inside the icing, release the pressure and pull the bag slightly along the cake. Squeeze the bag again to expel more icing, release and pull (14). Continue along the cake.

By changing the nozzles you get different effects. In the photograph above, you can see the difference between a plain and a star nozzle.

Incorporating candles

Candles are such an important part of a birthday cake that they really need to be thought about right at the beginning of the design stage to make sure that there's room for them. Yet often they are not considered until five minutes before the cake is bought out.

If you make your own candleholders out of sugarpaste then, not only can you be sure that they will fit in with the design, but you can also sit the candles around the board. Make sure both the holders and candles are stuck down safely and securely (you can use a dab of royal icing to be extra sure) and that nothing is overhanging or too close to the flames.

To make rock or pebble holders which are useful for all kinds of cake designs, partially knead a little black and white sugarpaste together to get a marbled effect. Pull off small pieces and roll into chunks. Stick into position and insert a candle in the centre (15).

Small balls of sugarpaste also make ideal candleholders and are easy to make. For something more decorative, roll out some icing about 1 cm (⅜ in) thick and cut out a shape, such as a flower or a star, with a cutter.

Space-fillers

Simple cartoon-style flowers make useful space fillers on cakes and are quick and easy to make. Use a "five petal flower" cutter which you can find at any cake decorating equipment shop. Cut out a flower shape and stick a flattened ball of yellow sugarpaste in the centre (16). Alternatively, you could cut out a series of small discs using something such as a piping nozzle. Arrange them in a circle and again finish off with a yellow sugarpaste centre.

Basic Equipment

Baking tins (pans) A good assortment of shapes and sizes is useful.

Board Useful when modelling small sugarpaste items.

Bread knife A long, sharp serrated knife is essential for shaping and slicing cakes.

Cake smoothers By using a smoother like an iron, and running it over the surface of a covered cake, small bumps and lumps can literally be ironed out. Essential for achieving a smooth professional finish (see page 9).

Cocktail sticks (toothpicks) These can be used as supports inside models, for adding food colour to sugarpaste, and for making frills and dotty patterns.

Cooling rack Available in all shapes and sizes and used for cooling cakes.

Cutters A vast range is available in both plastic and metal.

Drinking straws These can be used as tiny circle cutters and are ideal for making eyes. Held at an angle and pressed into sugarpaste, they can also be used for making the scales on snakes or dinosaurs.

Greaseproof (waxed) paper Used for lining tins, making piping bags, storing fruit cakes, and in place of tracing paper.

Measuring spoons A set of standard spoons ensures that you use the same quantities each time you re-make a recipe.

Mixing bowls Even the simplest cake uses more than one bowl, so a good selection of bowls is useful.

Paintbrushes A selection of various sizes is useful. A medium brush is good for sticking things with water when modelling, and a fine brush for adding delicate detail. Although more expensive, sable brushes are the best.

Palette knife (metal spatula) For spreading jam or buttercream, mixing colour into larger quantities of royal icing, and lifting small bits of sugarpaste.

Piping nozzles or tubes A varied selection is always useful and they can always double up as small circle cutters. Metal nozzles are more expensive than plastic but are sharper and more accurate.

Rolling pin A long rolling pin will not leave handle dents in the sugarpaste. Tiny ones are also available and are handy for rolling out small quantities of sugarpaste when modelling. If you don't possess a small rolling pin, a paintbrush handle will often do the job just as well.

Ruler Not just for measuring, a ruler can also be useful for pressing lines and patterns into sugarpaste.

Scalpel Invaluable when careful cutting is required, such as a template.

Scissors A decent pair of sharp scissors is essential for making piping bags, cutting linings for tins, and sometimes sugarpaste.

Sieve (sifter) Vital for sifting flour and icing sugar. Also a useful tool for making bushes or hair by simply pushing a lump of sugarpaste through the mesh.

Small dishes Useful for holding water when modelling, icing sugar when rolling out sugarpaste. Also ideal when mixing food colour into royal icing.

Small sharp knife A small kitchen knife with a sharp, straight blade will become one of your most important pieces of equipment.

Soft pastry brush It is useful to have two – for dampening or cleaning large areas, and for brushing away dusty fingerprints or specks of dried sugarpaste.

Tape measure Useful for measuring cakes and boards to ensure that you have rolled out enough sugarpaste.

Turntable Although not strictly speaking essential, once you've used one, you'll wonder what you ever did without it. Cheaper versions are available in plastic.

Wooden spoon As well as mixing, the handle can be used as a modelling tool.

RULER

MEASURING SPOON

SIEVE (SIFTER)

MIXING BOWL

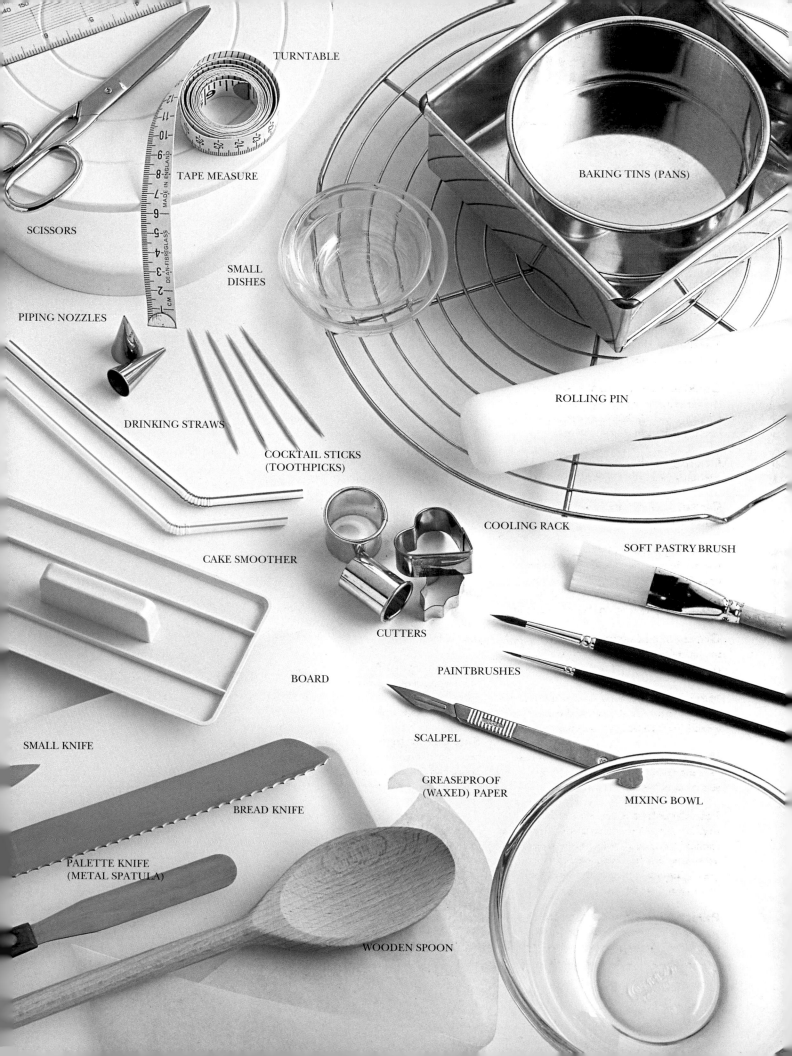

TURNTABLE

TAPE MEASURE

SCISSORS

SMALL DISHES

BAKING TINS (PANS)

PIPING NOZZLES

ROLLING PIN

DRINKING STRAWS

COCKTAIL STICKS
(TOOTHPICKS)

COOLING RACK

SOFT PASTRY BRUSH

CAKE SMOOTHER

CUTTERS

PAINTBRUSHES

BOARD

SMALL KNIFE

SCALPEL

GREASEPROOF
(WAXED) PAPER

MIXING BOWL

BREAD KNIFE

PALETTE KNIFE
(METAL SPATULA)

WOODEN SPOON

Cakes

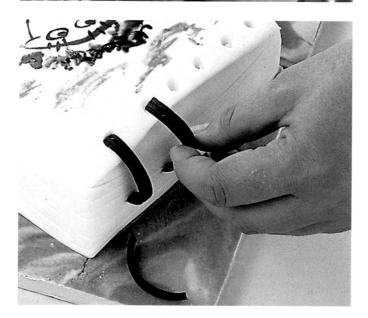

If you have children, then the Fairytale Castle (page 32), the Caterpillar cake (page 102), the Gingerbread cake (page 120) and the Wicked Witch (page 123) will be of special interest indeed. These are fun cakes, designed especially for children to put together with just a little bit of adult help and guidance.

Although, having said that, when they see how easy sugarpaste (rolled fondant) is to use, they'll probably want to help make all the rest of the cakes as well! There are plenty of cakes for all occasions, from Christmas and Easter to birthdays and Mother's Day.

Fairy-tale castle

Although this cake is a lot easier to make than it looks, you do have to allow drying time for the turrets (preferably overnight). Once you have mastered gelatin icing, a whole new world of standing models opens up.

1 Begin by making the turrets. Cover all the cardboard tubes with cling film and dust lightly with cornflour. Make up the gelatin icing as shown on page 15 and place in a polythene bag. Dust the worksurface with cornflour. Pull off a lump of icing about 130 g (4¼ oz) and roll out no thicker than 3 mm (⅛ in). Cut out a rectangle about 14 cm x 16 cm (5½ in x 6½ in). Place the excess icing back in the bag.

Wrap the icing round one of the thicker tubes and secure the join with a little water *(fig 1)*. Place to dry (seam side down) on a spare cake board or similar. Make another four the same size and one shorter one using the thinner tube. The smaller turret should be about 8 cm (3 in) in length.

After about 4-6 hours of drying, the turrets should feel hard on the outside. Carefully slide them off their supports and stand them upright so the centres can dry out. Leave overnight.

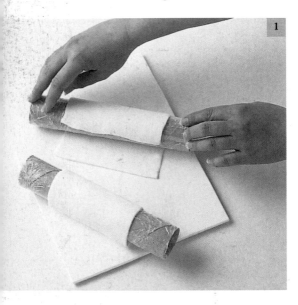

2 Level the top of the cake and place it upside down in the middle of the board. Slice and fill the centre with buttercream. Spread a thin layer of buttercream over the top and sides.

3 Dust the worksurface with icing sugar. Roll out and cover the cake with 500 g (1 lb 2 oz) of white sugarpaste. Smooth the top and sides and trim any excess from the base. Press a clean ruler horizontally three or four times around the sides of the cake *(fig 2)*. Then use the back of a knife to make the vertical marks for the bricks.

4 When dry, place a long and short turret together on top of the cake. Ensure the seams are at the back and secure them using royal icing. To provide extra support, roll 30 g (1 oz) of white sugarpaste into a sausage about 28 cm (11 in) long. Paint a light line of water around the base of the two turrets and, starting from the back, press the sausage in place *(fig 3)*.

5 To make two doors, thinly roll out the brown sugarpaste and cut out two rounded, arched shapes. Press a few vertical lines into each one with the back of a knife. Stick the largest door on the front of the cake and the other on the front of the tallest turret. Make two steps in front of each door by sticking two small ovals of white sugarpaste

■ INGREDIENTS

- 1 quantity gelatin icing (see page 20)
- Cornflour (cornstarch)
- 18 cm (7 in) round sponge cake
- 1 quantity buttercream (see page 19)
- Icing (confectioners') sugar
- 700 g (1 lb 8 oz) white sugarpaste (rolled fondant)
- 10 g (¼ oz) brown sugarpaste (rolled fondant)
- 40 g (1¾ oz) black sugarpaste (rolled fondant)
- 1 quantity white royal icing (see page 20)
- 2 edible silver balls
- 25 mini marshmallows
- 6 ice cream cones
- Two 30 g (1 oz) bags white chocolate buttons or similar
- Green food colour (ideally gooseberry green but not essential)
- 1 sheet rice paper
- 70 g (2½ oz) green-coloured coconut (see page 20)

■ UTENSILS

- 6 cardboard tubes (5 paper towel inner tubes and one from a roll of tin foil are ideal. Please don't use toilet rolls!)
- Cling film (plastic wrap)
- Rolling pin
- Small sharp knife
- Water and paintbrush
- Carving knife
- 30 cm (12 in) square cake board
- Ruler
- 4 piping (decorating) bags (minimum)
- Number 2 piping nozzle
- Scissors
- Small sieve

on top of each other *(fig 4)*. Stick an edible silver ball on the front of each door with a little royal icing.

6 Stick about 25 mini marshmallows around the perimeter of the cake with royal icing. (If you cannot find mini marshmallows in the supermarket, cut up a sausage of sugarpaste instead.)

7 Take two of the ice cream cones. Break little pieces off the base if necessary to help them stand upright. Pipe a thin line of royal icing around the top edges of both turrets and then stick the cones carefully in place on top.

You may find that you have to break a little 'bitc' shape out of one side of the cone that goes on top of the shorter turret

so that it can sit snugly against the taller turret *(fig 5)*.

8 Neaten the base of each cone with a line of white chocolate buttons stuck on with dabs of royal icing.

9 Place the four remaining gelatin cylinders around the cake. Secure with royal icing and top each one with a cone and line of buttons as before.

10 To make the windows on the turrets, thinly roll out the black sugarpaste and cut out eight narrow rectangles. Keep the leftover icing. Cut one end of each rectangle into a point. Stick one on each turret and two either side of the front door.

Place a little white royal icing in a piping bag fitted with the number 2 icing nozzle. Pipe a neat line from the top to the bottom of a window *(fig 6)*. Then pipe a line across the window. Repeat on all the rest. (Leave the windows bare if you find this too tricky.)

11 To make the rocks, partially knead together 100 g (4 oz) of white sugarpaste and 10 g (¼ oz) of black. Pull off irregular lumps and stick these on the board around the cake using a little water.

12 Colour 45 ml (3 tbsp) of royal icing green. Place half into a piping bag fitted with the number 2 piping nozzle and pipe wiggly lines for the ivy stems all over the cake. Place the rest of the icing in a second bag and snip 3 mm (⅛ in) off the end of the bag. Press the end of the bag against a stem, squeeze lightly then pull the bag away. This should make a simple leaf shape. Continue all over the cake. Practise this first on a sheet of greaseproof paper if you are not very confident.

13 To make the flags, cut six small triangles out of the sheet of rice paper. Pipe a dot of royal icing on the top of one of the cones. Stick a small ball of sugarpaste on top and pipe another dot on top of that. Press one of the triangles into the sugarpaste *(fig 7)*. Repeat on the other five cones.

14 Moisten the exposed cake board with a little water and sprinkle the coloured coconut around the base of the cake. To add snow, place a spoonful of icing sugar in a small sieve and sprinkle over the cake.

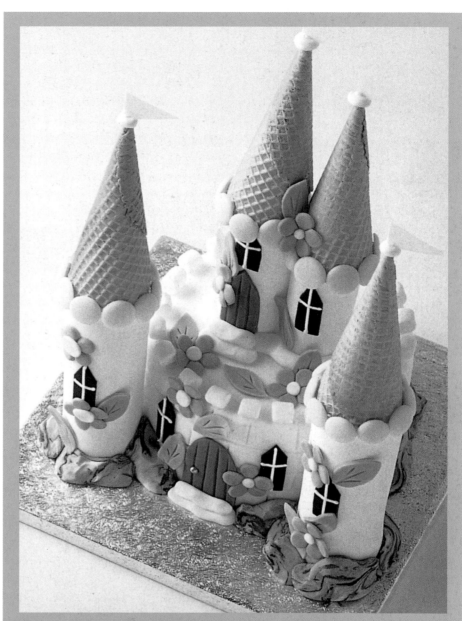

Decorating variation

In this simplified version there are only four turrets instead of six, which saves you time. Also, instead of piping leaves, I have used cut-out flowers and leaves which look just as good. You could also place little figures in front of the top turrets. Alternatively, you could use bride and groom figures and turn it into a stunning wedding cake with a difference.

Do-it-yourself

The ideal cake for anyone to who likes to wield a hammer or the perfect hint for someone you wish would! Give the sponge itself a 'wood' effect by partially mixing a couple of teaspoons of cocoa into the madeira mixture before it's cooked. Once baked, it should have an interesting marbled look to it.

INGREDIENTS

15 cm (6 in) square cake
1 quantity buttercream (see page 19)
60 g (2¼ oz) orange gelatin icing (see page 20)
50 g (2 oz) grey gelatin icing (see page 20)
600 g (1 lb 6 oz) white sugarpaste (rolled fondant)
20 g (¾ oz) grey sugarpaste (rolled fondant)
50 g (2 oz) red sugarpaste (rolled fondant)
50 g (2 oz) black sugarpaste (rolled fondant)
50 g (2 oz) tan sugarpaste (rolled fondant)
10 g (¼ oz) blue sugarpaste (rolled fondant)
20 g (¾ oz) orange sugarpaste (rolled fondant)
Royal icing, (optional, see page 20)
Cornflour (cornstarch)
Dark brown, chestnut and black food colours
Icing (confectioners') sugar, for rolling out
Water

UTENSILS

20 cm (8 in) square cake board
Templates for saw (page 141)
Scalpel
Spare cake board
Rolling pin
Carving knife
Sharp knife
Palette knife (metal spatula)
Cake smoothers
Paintbrushes, one medium, one fine

1 Roll out the grey gelatin icing to a thickness of 3 mm (⅛ in). Place the saw template onto the icing and cut out the shape using a scalpel. (Although a sharp knife will do the job adequately, it's a lot easier with a scalpel.)

2 Roll out the orange gelatin icing and, using the templates, cut out two handle shapes. Place the three gelatin icing pieces onto a spare cake board that has been lightly dusted with cornflour and leave to dry overnight.

3 Slice the top off the cake to level it and turn it upside down. Cut the cake in half and fill the centre with buttercream. Spread more buttercream around the sides and over the top.

4 Place the cake slightly off centre on the cake board so that there is a wider expanse of cake board showing at the front and on the right-hand side.

5 Put 20 g (¾ oz) of the white sugarpaste to one side. Carefully roll the dark brown and chestnut food colours into the icing to achieve a nice wood-grain effect (see page 19). Roll out the icing and cover the cake and smooth the sides. Trim away and keep the excess. Finish neatening the sides with a pair of cake smoothers.

6 Cut a thin strip out of the cake, ready for the saw, while the icing is still soft. Make a 5 mm (¼ in) wide cut from the base of the cake to about halfway across the top of the cake. Lift this section of cake out and discard *(fig 1)*.

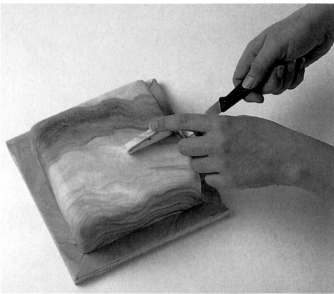

fig 1

7 Moisten the exposed cake board. Roll out the excess 'woodgrain' icing to a thickness of about 3 mm (⅛ in) and cut out four strips. Lay one strip down each edge. Trim to fit (see page 17).

8 Now make the tools *(fig 2)*. To make the screwdriver, roll 10 g (¼ oz) of grey sugarpaste into a sausage (rope) approximately 10 cm (4 in) long and squash one end. Make a small flattened grey ball, and place this against the blunt end. Make a handle by rolling the red sugarpaste into

fig 2

a pear shape. Place the screwdriver into position on the cake and adhere with a little water.

9 For the ruler, roll 20 g (¾ oz) of white sugarpaste into a flat strip and cut out a rectangle 13 cm x 2.5 cm (5 in x 1 in). Carefully paint on a few lines for markings with black food colour and a fine paint brush. Stick the ruler onto the cake.

10 To make the hammer, first roll the black sugarpaste into an exaggerated pear shape. Slice a strip off the larger end and place onto the cake board. For the handle, roll the tan sugarpaste into a slightly tapering sausage approximately 18 cm (7 in) long. Place the handle into position, and stick with a little water using the side of the cake as support.

11 For the pencil, roll the blue sugarpaste into a thin sausage about 10 cm (4 in) long. Stick this onto the cake board. Finish it off with a tiny cone of flesh-coloured icing and paint in a tiny point with black food colour.

12 To put the saw together, sandwich the grey blade between the two orange handles (*fig 3*). A little water should be enough to cement the sections together but if you find they won't stick, use a few dabs of royal icing. Lightly moisten the edge of the saw handle and the inside of the

hole. Roll out the orange sugarpaste into a strip and wind this round to neaten the appearance of the handle. Trim away any excess.

13 Put the saw into the slot.

TIP: *Make the saw at least a day before the rest of the cake so you won't have to wait for it to dry when everything else is ready.*

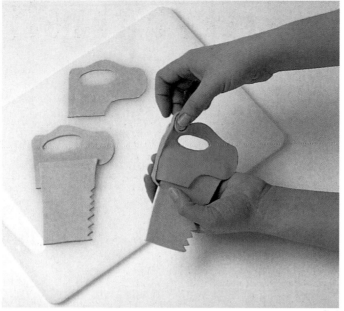
fig 3

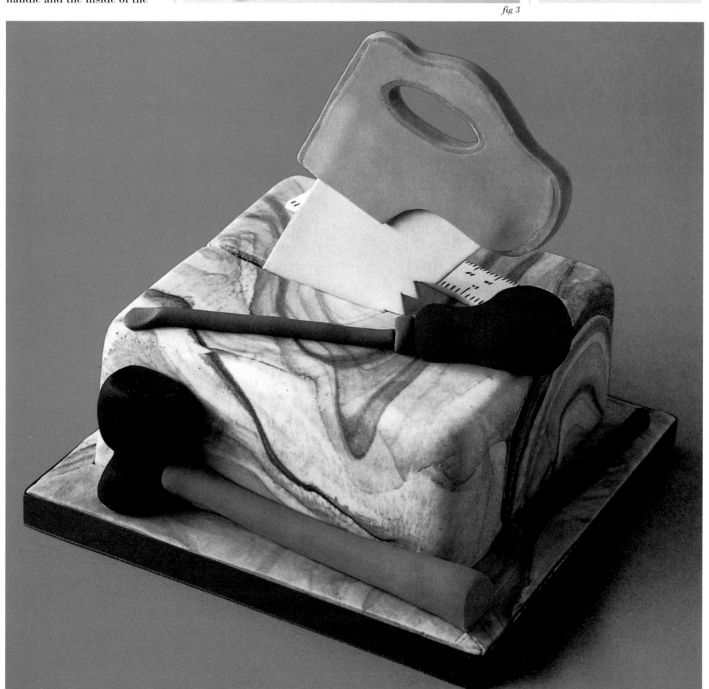

Spend, spend, spend

A dazzling cake piled up with gold coins that would suit either an accountant or someone who just likes to spend, spend, spend! This makes a nice cake for a man and let's face it, is a lot more original than a pair of socks! If you're making it for a woman, you might like to substitute small purses for the drawstring pouches.

INGREDIENTS

18 cm (7 in) square cake
1 quantity buttercream (see page 19)
500 g (1 lb 2 oz) emerald green sugarpaste (rolled fondant)
100 g (4 oz) dark brown sugarpaste (rolled fondant)
100 g (4 oz) light brown sugarpaste (rolled fondant)
10 g (¼ oz) red sugarpaste (rolled fondant)
10 g (¼ oz) blue sugarpaste (rolled fondant)
About 60 foil-covered chocolate coins
1 tbsp white royal icing (see page 20)
Icing sugar, for rolling out
Water

UTENSILS

25 cm (10 in) gold-coloured square cake board
Carving knife
Small sharp knife
Palette knife (metal spatula)
Rolling pin
Cake smoothers
Paintbrush
Piping bag fitted with a No 2 nozzle (round tip)

1 Slice off the top of the cake to level it and turn it upside down on the cake board so that the base now forms the top. Position the cake so that it sits off-centre on the board.

2 Slice the cake in half and fill it with buttercream. Spread buttercream over the top and down the sides with a palette knife.

3 Knead the emerald green sugarpaste and roll it out. Carefully cover the cake.

4 Smooth the sugarpaste over the top and sides with your hands and trim away any excess icing at the base. Then run over the surface of the icing using a pair of cake smoothers.

5 To make a purse, take the dark brown icing and mould it into a cone shape (*fig 1*). Push your finger into the top of the thin end to make a slight hollow. This will become the opening of the purse. Pinch the edges around the top of the hollow to thin them slightly and bend them outwards. Squeeze the neck of the purse to re-shape it as necessary. Stand the purse in position on the cake. Repeat with the

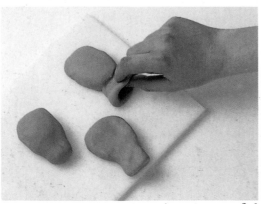

fig 1

lighter brown icing but this time lay it flat on the cake instead of standing up.

6 Begin to position the coins

fig 2

around the cake, securing them into position with royal icing (*fig 2*).

7 Finish off the purses by adding a drawstring. Poke the pointed end of a paintbrush around the neck of each purse to leave a line of small dots. (Make approximately 6-7 holes per purse about 1 cm (½ in) apart.) Using the piping bag and No 2 nozzle (round tip), pipe a line of icing between two of the holes. Leave a gap and pipe another line between the next two holes (*fig 3*). This should give the impression of a cord being threaded through.

8 Make two tiny red balls and two tiny blue ones out of icing. Stick the two red ones on the neck of the standing up purse. Pipe two 'tails' of icing away from them. On the lying down

purse, pipe the 'tails' before adding the blue balls to look as though the purse has fallen slightly open.

9 Finish arranging the coins around the cake and board.

fig 3

TIP: *It's always worth stocking up with chocolate coins at Christmas when they are more readily available in the shops. You never know when you might need some!*

Teatime table

There are a number of ways you can cheat with this cake and yet still produce something spectacular and unique. If you don't fancy making a gelatin plate (or you haven't got the time to wait for it to dry) simply use a real one instead and pile it up with home-made (or shop-bought) goodies you know the family will love.

1 Cover the china plate with clingfilm and a fine dusting of cornflour.

2 Roll out the gelatin icing and cover the plate. Trim the edges. Leave to dry for at least 24 hours, turning the icing plate over when it has hardened enough to support itself.

3 Level the top of the cake and turn it upside down on to the cake board. Slice it in half and fill the centre with buttercream. Reassemble the cake and spread additional buttercream around the top and sides.

4 Knead and roll out the white sugarpaste. Place it over the cake and cover it. Smooth down the top and sides with cake smoothers and trim away any excess.

5 Knead and roll out the pink sugarpaste to a thickness of about 5mm (¼ in). Using the larger cake board or equivalent as a template, cut out a circle.

6 Lay the pink icing on top of the white and allow it to fall into folds down the sides (*fig 1*).

7 Using the end of a paintbrush, poke a pattern into the edges of the cloth (*fig 2*).

8 When the plate is dry, place it on top of the tablecloth.

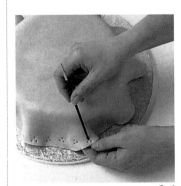

fig 2

9 Put the royal icing into a piping bag and snip off the end. Decorate the edge of the plate with small jelly sweets (candies). Secure them into position with the royal icing (*fig 3*).

10 Fill the plate with small cakes, biscuits or whatever takes your fancy.

TIP: *To ensure that the plate does not crack when you turn it over to dry the underside, place some scrunched up clingfilm under the plate to provide support.*

Secure it firmly with a dab of royal icing.

fig 1

fig 3

Fairy Town

If there are lots of children coming to the party, you may find that you have to make a few extra toadstools – they look so cute that everyone will want to take one home with them.

1 Begin by carving the cake into a slightly irregular shape by cutting slight slopes and hollows out of it. Then slice the cake horizontally in half and fill with a layer of buttercream. Reassemble and place in the centre of the cake board. Spread a thin layer of buttercream over the outside of the cake. Break and roll 30 g (1 oz) white sugarpaste into four rounded ball shapes. Stick these onto the board around the cake (1).

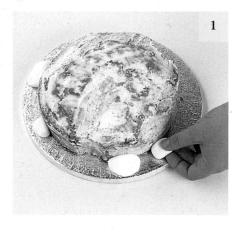

2 Lightly moisten both the cake board and the positioned sugarpaste balls with a little water. Dust your worksurface with icing sugar and knead 700 g (1 lb 9 oz) white sugarpaste until soft and pliable.

Roll out the icing to a width of about 36 cm (14 in). Lift and place over both the cake and the board. Starting from the top of the cake, smooth and press the icing into position. Trim and neaten the edges.

Carol suggests

Don't panic if for some reason your icing won't cover the entire cake and board in one go. Cover as much as you can and hide gaps, tears or creases with leaves and pebbles later.

3 For the toadstools, take one 45 g (1½ oz) lump and three 30 g (1 oz) lumps of white sugarpaste and mould each piece into a shape like a light bulb (2). Make the base and top of each "light bulb" fairly flat so that they stand securely and support the roof shape.

4 Using a little brown food colour, paint and fill in an arch shape for a front door (see page 24 for tips on painting with food colour). Then paint the outline with black food colour paste. Add a few vertical lines and a dot for the handle. (If you paint the black outline in first, it will simply bleed into the brown.) Still using the black, paint a small arch either side of the door for the windows. Add a small rectangle for the windowsill and a cross for the windowpanes. Repeat on the other toadstools.

5 Stick the toadstool bases on the cake with a little water. Check that they're sitting securely and dab a little water on the top of each one. To make the roofs, divide the red sugarpaste into four pieces. Roll each piece into a flattish disc shape and pinch around the outside edges to thin them. Stick one roof on each toadstool.

Roll tiny little bits of white sugarpaste into minute balls and flatten them to make the spots on the roofs. Stick four or five on each roof.

For the chimneys, roll the black sugarpaste into a thin sausage. Cut off the rounded ends and cut four short, stubby lengths. Stick one on each toadstool roof. Top each chimney base with a tiny triangle rolled out of the leftover black sugarpaste.

Carol suggests

If you are unsure about painting, substitute tiny sugarpaste cut-outs instead for the windows and doors.

INGREDIENTS

- 20 cm (8 in) round sponge cake (see page 14)
- 1 quantity buttercream (see page 19)
- 960 g (2 lb 2 oz) white sugarpaste (rolled fondant)
- Icing (confectioners') sugar for rolling out
- Brown, black and gooseberry green food colour pastes
- 45 g (1½ oz) red sugarpaste (rolled fondant)
- 5 g (⅛ oz) black sugarpaste (rolled fondant)
- 35 g (1⅛ oz) pink sugarpaste (rolled fondant)
- 5 g (⅛ oz) blue sugarpaste (rolled fondant)
- 30 g (1 oz) light green sugarpaste (rolled fondant)
- 30 g (1 oz) dark green sugarpaste (rolled fondant)
- 10 g (¼ oz) yellow sugarpaste (rolled fondant)
- 5 g (⅛ oz) flesh-coloured sugarpaste (rolled fondant)
- 1 tbsp yellow-coloured buttercream or royal icing (see page 19–20)
- 1 sheet rice paper

UTENSILS

- Carving knife
- 25 cm (10 in) round cake board
- Palette knife (metal spatula)
- Rolling pin
- Paintbrush
- Small sharp knife
- Pastry brush
- Piping (decorating) bag (see page 26)
- Scissors

6 Using a large soft brush, such as a pastry brush, dab some watered-down gooseberry green food colour over and around the cake. (Feel free to substitute another shade of green if you don't have gooseberry.)

7 For the pebbles, take two 45 g (1½ oz) lumps of white sugarpaste and 5 g (⅛ oz) pink and 5 g (⅛ oz) blue sugarpaste. Partially knead the pink into one piece of white and the blue into the other to get a marbled effect (see page 8). Pull bits off both pieces and roll into small pebble shapes. Keep about 5–10 g (⅛ – ¼ oz) of each colour for making the fairies' bodies later. Stick the pebbles around the cake and board (3).

8 To make the leaves, thinly roll out both the dark green and the light green sugarpaste. Cut out some very basic leaf shapes (3) using the tip of your knife and stick around the cake using water. (This is an ideal time to cover up any cracks or watermarks on the white sugarpaste.) Scrunch and re-roll the icing as necessary.

9 To make the flowers, use 30 g (1 oz) pink sugarpaste and the yellow sugarpaste. (Instructions for making these are in the Basic Techniques section on page 27.)

10 To make a fairy, first roll either a tiny bit of pale blue or pale pink sugarpaste into a tiny triangle (2). Add a tiny ball of flesh-coloured sugarpaste for the head and tiny sugarpaste marbled strings for the arms and legs. Place the fairies around the cake.

11 Paint two tiny black dots on each face for the fairy's eyes and place a tablespoon of yellow-coloured butter-cream or royal icing into a piping bag (see page 26 for instructions on making a piping bag). Snip a tiny triangle off the end of the bag and pipe an abundance of squiggly hair onto each fairy.

Finally, for the fairies' wings, cut some tiny heart shapes out of a sheet of rice paper. Bend each heart in half and press onto a fairy's back. As it dries, the hair should hold it in place.

Carol suggests

If a fairy is peeking out from behind a toadstool or from under a leaf, then you don't need to make her legs or wings as they won't be seen.

Candles

Stick your candles into the icing pebbles around the cake. Be sure to keep them away from the fairies' wings and any overhanging toadstool roofs.

Yacht

A fun cake for anyone who fancies themselves as a bit of a sailor. Paint the recipient's name or age on the sails and if they actually own their own boat, copy those colours. Have fun with the sea as well. Add jelly (candy) or icing fish or, if your sense of humour veers toward the wicked, maybe a shark's fin or two.

fig 1

1 Cut out the shape of the boat from the sponge (*fig 1*). Use strips cut from the discarded edges of the sponge to increase the boat's length. Carefully carve the sides of the cake so that they slope gently inwards and give the boat a nice rounded look. Slice and fill the centre with buttercream, then spread it around the top and sides.

2 Roll out 450 g (1 lb) red sugarpaste on a surface dusted with icing sugar. Cut out a strip approximately 50 cm (20 in) long and 5 cm (2 in) wide. (This last measurement depends on the depth of your cake so measure it first before cutting.) Roll the strip up like a bandage and starting from the straight edge at the back of the boat, unwind it around the base of the boat. Neaten the sides using smoothers and trim away any excess icing at the join (seam). Ensure that the top edge of the icing lies level with the top of the cake, trimming it if necessary.

3 To give the impression of boards around the boat, take a ruler and holding it horizontally, press the edge two or three times into both sides of the boat.

(A photograph showing this technique appears in "Enchanted House" page 76.)

4 Thinly roll out 100 g (4 oz) black sugarpaste and cut out a shape slightly larger than the top of the boat. Lay the sugarpaste on the top of the boat and run a knife around the edge to trim it to size. Roll out 100 g (4 oz) red sugarpaste and cut out two strips for the boat's seats approximately 2.5 cm (1 in) wide. Lightly moisten the black sugarpaste with a little water and place them into position.

5 Roll 100 g (4 oz) of red sugarpaste icing into a sausage about 60 cm (24 in) long. Moisten the top edge of the boat with water and lay the strip into position (*fig 2*).

6 Shape 90 g (3 ½ oz) white sugarpaste into an oval for the sailor's body. Thinly roll out

25 g (1 oz) of blue sugarpaste and cut out three thin strips about 15 cm (6 in) long. Moisten the body and wrap them round to make stripes. Make two arms out of 25 g (1 oz) blue sugarpaste. Bend them slightly at the elbow and stick onto the body with water (*fig 3*). Place the sailor into position and secure with a little water. For extra security, carefully push the smaller wooden skewer through the body into the cake, leaving about 2.5 cm (1 in) protruding. Roll 10 g (¼ oz) flesh-colored sugarpaste into a ball for the head. Moisten the neck and slide the head into position over the skewer.

To make the sailor's facial hair ('de rigeuer' for any self-respecting seaman!) take the remaining black sugarpaste. Make a tiny triangle for the beard and stick on to the face. Add two tiny black ovals for the

fig 2

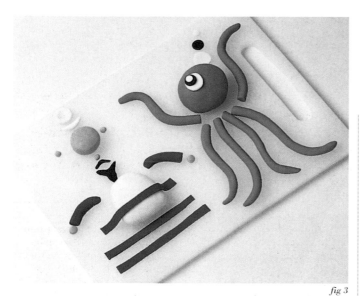

fig 3

made out of two balls of flesh-coloured sugarpaste.

7 For the octopus, make a 100g (4 oz) ball of green sugarpaste for the head and five 50 g (2 oz) green sausages for the legs (*fig 3*).

8 Place 5 tbsp of royal icing in a bowl and partially mix in a small amount of blue food colour. Using a palette knife, swirl the icing around the cake board. Position the octopus' head and legs, making sure the 'sea' covers the tops of the legs.

9 Stick two white circles of icing onto the octopus' face.

Add two smaller black ones. Finish off with two tiny white flattened dots of white to make the highlights. Paint in a mouth and two eyebrows with black food colour.

10 Attach the sails to the second wooden skewer with sticky tape. Finally insert them into the boat.

TIP: *If you go too far mixing the blue food colour into the 'sea' and it all turns blue, don't panic! Simply add more white royal icing to reverse the process.*

moustache. Stick a small flattened circle of white sugarpaste onto the top of his head to make his cap and finish it off with a tiny white oval of icing stuck to the front to make a peak. Add

three tiny balls of flesh-coloured icing for the ears and nose and paint in the eyes, hair and a dot for the mouth with black food colour and a fine paintbrush. Finish the arms with hands

Passing exams

A cake that shows how proud you are of someone's academic achievements. You could also write their name or the subject they passed on the certificate. If you can't get hold of ready-coloured black sugarpaste and have to colour your own, invest in some disposable polythene gloves to save discolouring your hands.

INGREDIENTS

18 cm (7 in) round cake
1 quantity buttercream (see page 19)
400 g (14 oz) white sugarpaste (rolled fondant)
900 g (2 lb) black sugarpaste (rolled fondant)
50 g (2 oz) red sugarpaste (rolled fondant)
100 g (4 oz) green sugarpaste (rolled fondant)
10 g (¼ oz) yellow sugarpaste (rolled fondant)
10 g (¼ oz) blue sugarpaste (rolled fondant)
Paprika
Dark brown food colour
Icing (confectioners') sugar, for rolling out
Water

UTENSILS

30 cm (12 in) round cake board
20 cm (8 in) thin, square cake board
Spare cake board
Carving knife
Small sharp knife
Palette knife (metal spatula)
Rolling pin
Cake smoothers
Fish slice (pancake turner)
Paintbrush
Cocktail stick (toothpick)
Small plastic bags

1 Knead paprika and dark brown food colour into 250 g (9 oz) white sugarpaste (rolled fondant icing) to achieve the wood grain effect as shown on page 10.

2 Moisten the 30 cm (12 in) cake board and cover it with the 'wood' icing (see page 21). Put the board to one side.

3 Turn the cake upside down on a spare cake board or clean work surface (countertop) and round the edges with a carving knife. Place the thinner cake board on top just to check that it sits nice and flat.

4 Slice the cake in half and fill the centre with buttercream. Cover the top and sides with buttercream.

5 Knead and roll out 500 g (1 lb 2 oz) of black sugarpaste and cover the cake with it. Smooth and trim away any excess.

6 Moisten the thin cake board with a little water. Roll out the remaining black sugarpaste and use this to cover the board.

7 Lift the round base cake using a fish slice or equivalent and place in the centre of the covered cake board.

8 Lightly moisten the top of the cake and place the thin black cake board into position on the top (*fig 1*).

9 Make a scroll out of 150 g (5 oz) white sugarpaste. Knead and roll it out and cut out a rectangle about 18 cm x 13 cm (7 in x 5 in) long. Roll it up and stick it onto the board with a little water.

fig 2

10 Cut out two thin red strips of sugarpaste and stick onto the scroll. Add a bow made out of another two red strips folded into two loops, two 'tails' and a small strip to cover the centre (*fig 2*).

11 Take the green sugarpaste. Pull off a small ball and put it to one side. Roll the rest into a tapering sausage (rope) shape approximately 23 cm (9 in) long. Flatten the sausage slightly and score lines down its length using the back of a knife (*fig 3*). Moisten the top of the mortar board and lay the tassel upon it, allowing the icing to rest on the board at the base. Add a few thin

strings of green sugarpaste to look like 'stragglers'.

12 Put the leftover ball of green sugarpaste on top and again score lines in it with the back of a knife.

13 For the pencils, simply roll the yellow sugarpaste and blue sugarpaste into 12 cm (5 in) lengths. Add a tiny brown cone to one end and a tiny flattened ball of white to the other. Paint in the leads with black food colour.

TIP: *Clean away dusty icing (confectioners') sugar fingerprints with clean water and a damp paintbrush.*

fig 3

fig 1

Valentine lips

If, as they say, the way to a man's (or woman's) heart is through their stomach, what better way to get there than by presenting them with this stylish, eye-catching cake. Gold cake boards are easily available from cake decorating equipment shops, and really set off the black and red icing.

INGREDIENTS

25 cm (10 in) square cake
2 quantities of buttercream
(see page 19)
1.25 kg (2 lb 12 oz) red
sugarpaste (rolled fondant)
50 g (2 oz) black sugarpaste
(rolled fondant)
1 tbsp black royal icing (see
page 20)
Icing (confectioners') sugar,
for rolling out
Water

UTENSILS

30 cm (12 in) square gold cake
board
Cake template (see page 140)
Carving knife
Small sharp knife
Palette knife (metal spatula)
Rolling pin
Cake smoothers
Small heart-shaped cutter
Piping (decorating) bag and
No 3 piping nozzle (round tip)
Paintbrush

fig 1

1 Cut out the cake using the template as a guide *(fig 1)*.

2 Round the sides and make sure that the outside edges of the lips slope downwards towards the board. Cut a groove along the middle *(fig 2)*. Position the cake on the board.

3 Slice and fill the centre with buttercream. Reassemble and cover the outside of the cake with buttercream.

4 Knead and roll out all the red sugarpaste to a thickness of 1 cm (½ in). (If it's nice and thick, it's easier to achieve a nice smooth luxurious finish.)

5 Lift and place the icing over the cake. Carefully press the icing into the groove. Then smooth and trim the sides, keeping the excess icing.

Finish off by running over the cake with a pair of smoothers.

6 Cut out two red heart shapes and make three sets of lips out of the leftover icing *(fig 3)*. For each pair of lips make two small red sausage (rope) shapes the same size. Make a small dent in the middle of the top lid and press the two sections together. Tweak the ends into points.

7 Thinly roll out the black sugarpaste and cut out eleven heart shapes using the cutter.

8 Arrange the hearts and lips around the cakes with squiggles of black royal icing.

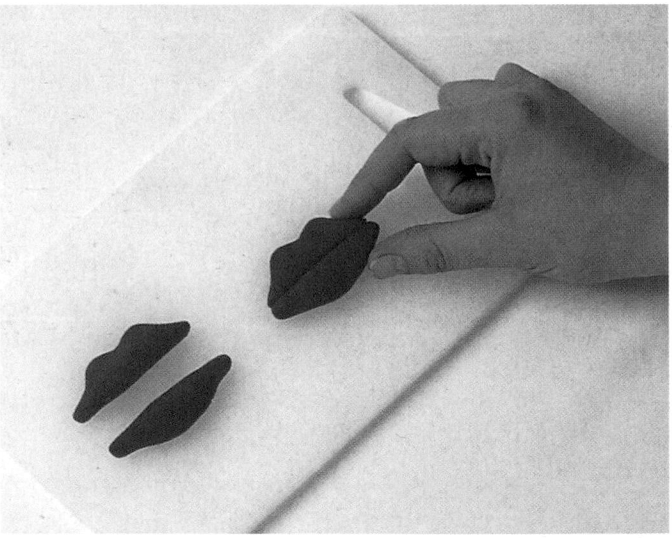

fig 3

TIP: *To save you time and effort on baking day, the small decorative lips and the hearts can easily be made a few days in advance. Store them carefully in an airtight tin until required.*

fig 2

Computer game

The perfect cake with which to tempt junior away from his computer game for a while. If you don't feel competent about painting onto the screen, substitute a photograph or a picture cut out of a comic or magazine instead. Stick it onto a thin bit of cardboard and secure onto the cake with a little royal icing.

INGREDIENTS

18 cm (7 in) square cake
1 quantity buttercream (see page 19)
400 g (14 oz) black sugarpaste (rolled fondant)
800 g (1 lb 12 oz) blue sugarpaste (rolled fondant)
50 g (2 oz) grey sugarpaste (rolled fondant)
20 g (¾ oz) red sugarpaste (rolled fondant)
10 g (¼ oz) yellow sugarpaste (rolled fondant)
black food colour
Icing (confectioners') sugar, for rolling out
Water

UTENSILS

25 cm (10 in) square cake board
Carving knife
Small sharp knife
Palette knife (metal spatula)
Rolling pin
Cake smoothers
Fish slice (pancake turner)
Circle cutters or equivalent
Paintbrushes, one medium, one fine

1 Cover the cake board with 350 g (12 oz) black sugarpaste (see page 21). Put the board to one side.

fig 1

2 Cut about a third off one side of the cake. Place the cut off section against one of the shorter sides of the cake to increase the length of the cake *(fig 1)*. Trim to fit.

3 Cut a small semi-circle out of one of the longer sides and place this against the opposite side of the cake *(fig 2)*.

4 Run a sharp knife around the edges of the cake to make them rounded.

5 Slice the cake in half and fill the centre with buttercream. Spread buttercream over the top and sides with a palette knife.

6 Knead the blue sugarpaste until pliable. Roll it out and cover the cake. Smooth the sides with cake smoothers and trim away any excess.

7 Carefully lift the cake using a fish slice and place it diagonally on the black sugarpasted cake board.

8 Roll out the grey sugarpaste and cut out a rectangle for the screen 7.5 cm x 5 cm (3 in x 2 in). Stick this in the centre of the cake using a little water.

9 Using the back of a knife, indent five lines each side of the screen.

10 Thinly roll out the red sugarpaste and cut out two circles 4 cm (1 ½ in) in diameter. Stick one either side of the screen below the indented lines.

11 Paint the design onto the screen using black food colour and a fine paintbrush *(fig 3)*.

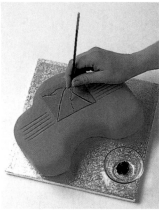

fig 3

12 Roll out the yellow sugarpaste and cut out a small cross and stick this onto one of the red circles. Stick a small yellow circle onto the other one. Cut out two yellow rectangles and one red one and stick these below the screen with a little water.

13 Roll 10 g (¼ oz) of black sugarpaste into a thin string and stick along the edge of the screen.

14 Roll the rest of the black sugarpaste into a slightly thicker string about 28 cm (11 in) long and lay this along the bottom edge of the game.

15 Roll out the rest of the blue sugarpaste and cut out about 16 circles. Use these to decorate the board.

TIP: *Add the ultimate psychedelic touch to the inside too by swirling a bit of food colour into the cake mixture before baking.*

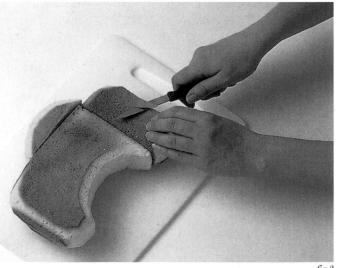

fig 2

Knapsack

Not only would this be an extremely apt cake for someone about to embark on a long voyage but it would also make a good cake for someone about to leave home for the first time. Alternatively, if they show no inclinations to fly the nest, you could make it as a cheeky hint that perhaps it was about time they did!

INGREDIENTS

15 cm (6 in) round cake
1 quantity buttercream (see page 19)
600 g (1 lb 6 oz) white sugarpaste (rolled fondant)
600 g (1 lb 6 oz) red sugarpaste (rolled fondant)
10 g (¼ oz) black sugarpaste (rolled fondant)
100 g (4 oz) green coloured sugar (see page 20)
2 breadsticks
Icing (confectioners') sugar, for rolling out on
Water

UTENSILS

25 cm (10 in) round cake board
Small sharp knife
Carving knife
Palette knife (metal spatula)
Rolling pin
Cake smoothers
Paintbrush

fig 1

1 Shape the cake. If it rose well in the oven, trim off the outside crust but keep most of the dome shape. Turn the cake upside down on the cake board. Round the sides and build up the height with approximately 250 g (9 oz) white sugarpaste (*fig 1*).

2 Split the cake and fill the centre with buttercream. Place onto the cake board and spread additional buttercream around the sides and top.

3 Knead and roll out the red sugarpaste and cover the cake with it. Smooth the sides with cake smoothers. Trim and keep the excess icing for making the tie later. Make a few crease marks with the back of a knife (*fig 2*).

4 Measure the breadsticks and cut to size. (It'll probably take about one and a half depending on the length of the sticks you use.)

5 For the tie, roll 50 g (2 oz) of red sugarpaste into a pointed oval shape about 10 cm (4 in) long. Pinch the centre together and flatten the whole shape slightly. Place on the top of the cake.

6 Place the breadsticks on top and twist the two sugarpaste ends over, making sure that the join in the breadsticks is hidden from view by the sugarpaste (*fig 3*).

7 Clean any dusty icing sugar marks off the cake with a damp paintbrush and a little water.

8 Divide 100 g (4 oz) of white sugarpaste into small flattened balls and stick onto the sides of the knapsack.

9 Make the rocks by partially kneading together the remaining white sugarpaste and the remaining black sugarpaste. Divide into misshapen balls and arrange on the board.

10 Finally moisten the cake board and carefully spoon the coloured sugar around the base of the cake.

fig 2

fig 3

TIP: *Don't make the red icing too moist when cleaning it with water or it will bleed.*

Wedding present

A bold way to decorate a single-tier cake. Tie the colours of the ribbons and mice in with the wedding colours and if you really fancy a challenge, find out what the bride and groom will be wearing and dress the mice in miniature replica outfits. Cake smoothers are essential for achieving the straight edges and neat corners required on this cake.

INGREDIENTS

30 cm (12 in) square fruit cake
2.5 kg (5 lb) marzipan
3.25 kg (7 lb 4 oz) white
sugarpaste (rolled fondant)
65 g (2 ½ oz) pink sugarpaste
(rolled fondant)
25 g (1 oz) black sugarpaste
(rolled fondant)
4 tbsp brandy
4 tbsp warmed apricot jam
White royal icing (see page 20)
Icing (confectioners') sugar
for rolling out
Black food colour
Water

UTENSILS

40 cm (16 in) square cake
board
Small sharp knife
Carving knife
Cocktail stick (toothpick)
Pastry brush
Rolling pin
Cake smoothers
Ruler
Heart-shaped cutters
Scissors
3 m (40 in) x 45 mm (1 ¾ in)
wide white ribbon
3 m (40 in) x 35 mm (1 ¼ in)
wide pink ribbon
3 m (40 in) x 25 mm (1 in) wide
white ribbon
3 m (40 in) x 15 mm (½ in) wide
pink ribbon
Piping bag
Paintbrushes, one medium,
one fine
Templates for mice clothes
(see page 141)

1 Level the top of the cake and place it upside down on the cake board. If there is a gap between what is now the base of the cake and the board, fill this with a sausage of marzipan. Pierce the cake a number of times with the cocktail stick and drizzle the brandy over the cake. Brush the warmed apricot jam over the top and sides using a pastry brush.

2 Place the marzipan onto a surface dusted with icing sugar. Knead it until it becomes nice and pliable then roll it out and cover the cake. Stroke the marzipan into place with your hands and trim away any excess from the base. Then run a pair of cake smoothers over the top and sides trying to get the corners as neat and squared as possible.

3 Moisten the marzipan with a little water to prepare for the next step.

4 Roll out 2.5 kg (5 lb) white sugarpaste. Lift the icing and carefully place it onto the cake. Smooth and trim the sides as necessary.

5 To make the folds in the paper, carefully press a long 'V' shape into two opposite sides of the cake using the edge of a clean ruler.

6 Press a heart-shaped cutter into the icing while it's still soft. This will make the pattern on the 'paper'. Take care not to press right into the fruit cake below as moisture from the fruit could leak through and discolour the cake (*fig 1*).

fig 1

7 Measure the height and width of the cake and cut two strips of the widest ribbon to that length (counting the height measurement twice). Arrange the two ribbons in a criss-cross fashion across the cake and secure the centre and the ends with dabs of royal icing. Don't worry if moisture from the icing leaks through the ribbon as this will be hidden by the bow and the icing round the board later. Repeat this procedure with the other three ribbon widths (*fig 2*).

8 To cover the board, thinly roll out 850 g (1 lb 14 oz) of white sugarpaste (see page 22). Cut this into strips wider than the width of the board. Moisten the exposed cake board with a little water. Take one of the strips and lay it onto the board, deliberately allowing it to fall into folds and creases as you do so. Continue to do this all around the cake, remembering to hide the ends of the ribbon. Trim away the excess from the edges and press down any gaping holes with your thumb.

fig 2

9 To make the groom, knead and roll 25 g (1 oz) pink sugarpaste into a cone shape *(fig 3)*. Bend the pointed end over to make a nose and flatten the base. Knead and roll out 10 g (¼ oz) black sugarpaste and cut out a jacket shape using the template if necessary. Wrap it around the groom's back and stick with a little water. Make a tiny black sausage for the arm and cut a tiny pea-sized ball of black sugarpaste in half for his feet. Give the groom a hat made out of a small black circle topped with a small black circle of icing.

10 For the bride, mould 20 g (¾ oz) of white sugarpaste into a small cone. Take another 10 g (¼ oz) oval of white sugarpaste and place this on top. Place a small pink pointed cone shape on top of this for her head. Make a small pink sausage of icing for the bride's arms and stick this onto the front of her body in a 'U' shape. Stick three tiny white balls onto her 'hands' and indent each ball with the tip of a paintbrush.

11 Give the bride a veil (see template, page 140) cut out of a rolled out bit of white icing. Stick this to the back of her head and finish off with three tiny white balls of icing on top.

Give each mouse two tiny balls for ears and indent each one with the tip of a paintbrush. On the faces, give each mouse two small flattened white circles for eyes and an even tinier one for the nose. Paint in the mouth, eyeballs and eyelashes with black food colour and a fine paintbrush.

12 Place the two mice into position and make two tails out of 20 g (¾ oz) of pink icing. Stick these into position.

13 Arrange the rest of the ribbon into an attractive bow and stick in place with a little royal icing.

TIP: *Wipe your hands after using the black sugarpaste so you don't get dirty fingerprints everywhere.*

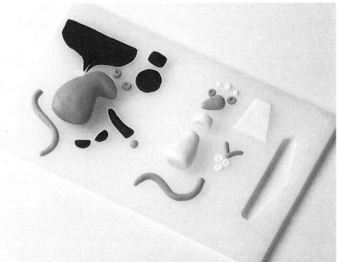

fig 3

Baby Dinosaur

Aah, this little guy looks almost too cute to eat and is very easy to make. If you want to incorporate candles into the design, do read the note at the end before you start making the cake.

1 If your cake rose a little too enthusiastically in the oven, you may need to take a slice away from the top so that it will sit comfortably and squarely upside-down on the cake board. Next, slice the cake horizontally a couple of times and sandwich the layers back together again with buttercream. Spread a thin covering of buttercream over the top and sides.

Roll out and cover the cake with the duck egg blue sugarpaste. Smooth the icing and trim around the base of the cake. Keep any excess and roll into little eggs for decorating the board or for use as candleholders.

2 Divide and roll about 30 g (1 oz) of both pale yellow and pink sugarpaste into small egg shapes.

3 Mix some blue food colour paste into some water. With a large soft brush, such as a pastry brush, flick and splatter the cake and the little eggs with the coloured water using light, controlled movements (1).

4 To make the baby dinosaur itself, begin with the head. Take 60 g (2 oz) pale yellow sugarpaste and roll into a thick sausage shape. Bend one end forwards to form the head. Press a dent using your finger across the head to make the dinosaur's forehead and ease the mouth area into a slightly pointed shape (2).

5 Stick two flattened ovals of white sugarpaste onto the head for his eyes. Paint the pupils, eyelashes and a mouth using black food colour.

6 Stick the head in position on top of the egg using a little water. Decorate the head and neck with a few scales made by pressing the edge of a drinking straw held at an angle into the icing to leave small "U" shape imprints.

7 Paint some cracks around the dinosaur using a little black food colour. Don't worry if you're hands are shaky – jagged, sudden movements will only make the cracks more authentic (3).

8 To make the arms, divide 10 g (¼ oz) pale yellow sugarpaste in half. Roll into two small sausage shapes. Squash and flatten one end of each sausage to make the hands and press a couple of lines into each hand using the back of a knife. Bend and stick the arms into position with a little water.

9 Use 30 g (1 oz) pale yellow sugarpaste for the tail. Roll it into a tapering sausage shape and stick onto the cake board. Paint a few cracks in the shell around the tail.

10 Moisten the exposed cake board and place the smaller eggs around the base of the cake. Carefully spoon the light brown sugar onto the board between the eggs.

Candles

If you want to use candles it would be better to use a larger board. Alternatively, position the cake towards the back of the board and insert your candles into the small eggs at the front.

INGREDIENTS

- 1 pudding bowl cake (see page 13)
- ⅓ quantity buttercream (see page 17)
- Icing sugar for rolling out
- 400 g (14 oz) duck egg blue sugarpaste (rolled fondant)
- 150 g (5¼ oz) pale yellow sugarpaste (rolled fondant)
- 30 g (1 oz) pale pink sugarpaste (rolled fondant)
- Blue and black food colour pastes
- 5 g (⅛ oz) white sugarpaste (rolled fondant)
- 45 g (1½ oz) light brown sugar

EQUIPMENT

- Carving knife
- Palette knife (metal spatula)
- 20 cm (8 in round cake board)
- Rolling pin
- Small sharp knife
- Pastry brush
- Paintbrush
- Drinking straw

NOTE: Make duck egg blue sugarpaste (rolled fondant) by mixing a little green (mint green) and blue (blueberry) food colour pastes into white sugarpaste. Or, you might be able to find a paste called "eucalyptus" which is ideal.

Valentine teddies

Teddies are extremely useful because they can be used on so many cakes. For example, a couple of brightly coloured ones would be ideal for a child whilst a big surly blue one bedecked with a tie might make a good gift for Father's Day. Although the ones featured here are fairly basic, you could always add some extra features.

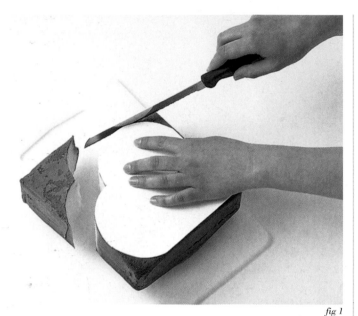

fig 1

1 Cut the cake to shape using the template *(fig 1)*. Level the top and place the cake upside down in the middle of the cake board.

2 Slice the cake and fill the centre with buttercream. Reassemble the cake and spread additional buttercream around the top and sides.

3 Knead and roll out the red sugarpaste (rolled fondant icing) fairly thickly. (Don't roll it any thinner than 1 cm (½ in).) Lift and place the icing over the cake and smooth the sides and trim away the excess. Run over the top and sides with cake smoothers.

4 To make the teddies, knead 75 g (3 oz) pink sugarpaste until pliable. Pull off a small ball (just enough to make four tiny ears later) and put this to one side. Divide the rest into two cone shapes. Bend them slightly so that they lean together. Add two 10 g (¼ oz) balls for heads.

For the legs, roll a 20 g (¾ oz) lump of sugarpaste into a sausage (rope) about 13 cm (5 in) long. Divide this into four. Flatten one end of each leg to make a foot and bend the foot up slightly to form a sort of 'L' shape. Lightly squeeze the thigh and place the legs into position. Poke the pointed end of a paintbrush, into the base of each paw four times to make the pads of the feet *(fig 2)*.

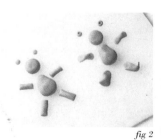

fig 2

5 Moisten the bears' stomachs with a little water and gently press the chocolates into position. Roll 10 g (¼ oz) pink icing into a sausage about 13 cm (5 in) long. Divide into four arms. Squeeze both ends

of each arm and stick onto the bodies with the hands clasping the chocolates *(fig 3)*. Give both teddies two small balls of pink for ears and poke a small hole in each one with the end of a paintbrush. Paint two small circles for eyes using black food colour and a fine paintbrush. Add pupils and also eyelashes on the lady. Stick two small flattened balls of white below the eyes for the muzzle. Paint a nose and mouth on each one.

fig 3

6 Roll a 50 g (2 oz) lump of white sugarpaste into small balls. Use these to decorate the edge of the cake. Stick them in place with water. Position the teddies. Roll out 100 g (4 oz) white sugarpaste and cut out 6 hearts with the cutter. Use these to decorate the cake.

7 Moisten the exposed cake board with water. Thinly roll out 200 g (7 oz) white sugarpaste. Cut this into strips and drape onto the board, coaxing the icing into irregular folds like material. Trim away the excess and press down any unsightly bits (see page 22).

TIP: *Assemble the teddies away from the cake so you don't lean on, and damage, the surface.*

Frog pond

In this cake, the pond is 'flooded' with royal icing. If you don't feel confident about trying this, simply cover the board with blue sugarpaste instead. The second new technique is modelling the waves out of piped royal icing. Don't worry if you're a bit unsure about handling a piping bag because the more wobbly the line the better.

INGREDIENTS

Heart-shaped cake cut out of a
18 cm (7 in) square cake using
the template on page 140
1 ½ quantities buttercream
(see page 19)
750 g (1 lb 10 oz) mid-green
sugarpaste (rolled fondant)
175 g (6 oz) dark green
sugarpaste (rolled fondant)
25 g (1 oz) yellow sugarpaste
(rolled fondant)
25 g (1 oz) black sugarpaste
(rolled fondant)
50 g (2 oz) white sugarpaste
(rolled fondant)
6 tbsp royal icing (see page 20)
Pink and blue food colours
Icing (confectioners') sugar,
for rolling out on
Water

UTENSILS

30 cm (12 in) round cake
board
Carving knife
Small sharp knife
Palette knife (metal spatula)
Rolling pin
Cake smoothers
Cocktail stick (toothpick) or
spaghetti
Piping (decorating) bag (with
uncut end)
Paintbrush
Small circle cutters or icing
nozzles (tips)
Piping bag (decorating) with
large nozzle inside (eg No 4 or
round tip)
Small bowls x 2
Small plastic bags

1 Slice the cake in half and fill the centre with buttercream. Place the cake on the board and cover the top and sides with buttercream as well.

2 Knead and roll out the mid-green sugarpaste (rolled fondant). Lift and place over the cake. Smooth the sides using your hands and a pair of cake smoothers and trim and keep any excess from the base.

3 Using the back of a knife, score a central vein down the centre of the leaf and add a couple leading away from it. Use about 10 g (¼ oz) of the leftover icing to make a sausage about 10 cm (4 in) long for the stem. Drape this from the back of the leaf onto the cake board.

4 Now make the frogs (*fig 1*). Make a 50 g (2 oz) ball of dark green sugarpaste for the male frog's body. Stick this onto the edge of the leaf and insert a cocktail (toothpick) stick or couple of strands of uncooked spaghetti.

fig 1

5 Moisten the neck and stick on a 25 g (1 oz) ball of dark green sugarpaste for the head.

6 To make the mouth, roll 10 g (¼ oz) of dark green sugarpaste into a longish oval

and press a line down the centre using the back of a knife. Tweak the ends and stick onto the head.

7 Make each leg out of 10 g (¼ oz) of green sugarpaste. Roll each one into a slightly tapered 10 cm (4 in) sausage (rope). Press and flatten about 2.5 cm (1 in) of the thicker end. The leg should now look like a small paddle. Cut 2 small triangles out of the foot to give the impression of webbed feet. Bend the leg into an 'S' shape and press against the frog's body, allowing the

end of the foot to just dangle over the side of the lily leaf. Repeat with the other foot.

8 For the lady frog, again make another 25 g (1 oz) ball of dark green sugarpaste for the head. Add a 10 g (¼ oz) strip for the mouth and score a line across the middle.

9 Make four small white sugarpaste balls and stick two

onto each frog for eyes. Add a small flattened circle of black to each eye and finish with a small ball of white for a highlight.

10 Add a little strip of yellow sugarpaste for Mrs Frog's hair. Cut out a pink bow and secure this to her head with a little water.

11 Divide 15 g (½ oz) dark green sugarpaste into four and make four small sausage-shaped arms, two for each frog. Secure these in position with a little water.

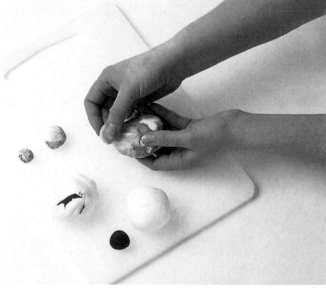

fig 2

12 Make the rocks by partially kneading 25 g (1 oz) black sugarpaste into 50 g (2 oz) white. Pull bits off and roll into small misshapen ball shapes (*fig 2*). Moisten the cake board and stick the rocks, close together, around the edge.

13 Put 5 tbsp royal icing into a small bowl. Stir in enough blue food colour to

make it a rich blue. Add just enough water so that when the knife is lifted out, the icing begins to fall back on itself and loses its shape. Spoon it into an empty piping bag. Snip the end off the bag and starting from the pointed end of the lily, begin to fill pool with 'water'. Move the piping bag from side to side across the exposed cake board in a wiggly motion. Push the icing into any reluctant corners with the tip of a damp paint

brush. Leave to dry for at least a few hours, or over night.

14 Make the lily flowers by cutting out 5 white petals per flower using a small circle cutter or piping nozzle (tip). Stick the petals around the lily pad. Now make yellow sugarpaste circles and stick these securely in the centre of each flower.

15 Put 1 tbsp white royal icing into a bag with No 4

fig 3

nozzle (tip). Pipe a line around base of the lily leaf. Using a damp paintbrush, stroke the icing back away from the leaf to achieve the wave effect (*fig 3*).

TIP: *Don't worry if you get a few trapped air bubbles in your 'flooded' water. They will enhance the pond by making it look authentic.*

Soccer

Colour the scarf in the recipient's favourite team's sporting colours and use it to hide any mistakes you might make when carving and covering the cake. If you really don't fancy the idea of shaping a rounded cake, it is possible to buy circular baking tins (pans) that do all the hard work for you.

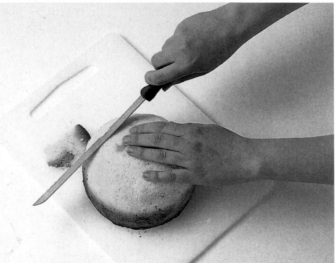

fig 1

fig 3

1 Carve the cake into a rounded dome shape (*fig 1*).

2 Slice the cake in half and fill the centre with buttercream. Continue to spread the buttercream around the top and sides. Place the cake in the centre of the board.

3 Knead and roll out half of the white sugarpaste and cover the cake. Trim away and keep any excess from the base. Run over the surface with a cake smoother.

4 Roll out the black sugarpaste and 200 g (7 oz) of white. Using the template and a scalpel or sharp knife, cut out 20 white hexagons and seven black hexagons.

5 Starting with a black hexagon in the centre of the cake, surround it with a circle of white ones. Build up the pattern, securing the hexagons with water (*fig 2*). When all the hexagons are in place, run over the surface with a cake smoother again to make them lie neat and flat.

6 Knead the remainder of the white sugarpaste until pliable. Roll it out and cut a strip about 50 cm x 7.5 cm (20 in x 3 in) to form the scarf.

7 Moisten the sides of the cake and wrap the scarf around (*fig 3*).

8 Roll out the blue sugarpaste and cut into stripes. Stick these onto the scarf securing them with water. Roll out and cut a white rectangle into a fringe. Stick onto the end of the scarf.

9 Moisten the exposed cake board and spoon the coloured sugar around the scarf.

TIP: *When you have cut out the hexagons, place a sheet of clingfilm (plastic wrap) over the top of them to stop them drying out and cracking before you stick them on.*

fig 2

Bouquet

The wonderful thing about this cake is its versatility. Not only would it make a lovely birthday cake but it could also be used for Mother's Day, Easter, Anniversaries or Valentine's Day. These roses are the fastest and easiest you'll ever see in icing. Colour them the recipient's favourite colour or, if rushed, use silk blooms instead.

INGREDIENTS

15 cm x 20 cm (6 in x 8 in) cake (Don't rush out to buy a special tin, simply trim a 20 cm (8 in) square cake instead.)
1 quantity buttercream (see page 19)
1 kg (2 lb 4 oz) white sugarpaste (rolled fondant)
50 g (2 oz) pale green sugarpaste (rolled fondant)
50 g (2 oz) mid-green sugarpaste (rolled fondant)
50 g (2 oz) dark green sugarpaste (rolled fondant)
100 g (4 oz) yellow sugarpaste (rolled fondant)
25 g (1 oz) violet sugarpaste (rolled fondant)
2 tbsp green royal icing (see page 20)
Icing (confectioners') sugar, for rolling out
Water

UTENSILS

35 cm (12 in) square cake board
Carving knife
Small sharp knife
Palette knife (metal spatula)
Rolling pin
Wooden spoon
Clingfilm (plastic wrap)
Paintbrush
Piping (decorating) bag with No 3 nozzle (round tip)
Tin foil
Cellophane (approximately 38 cm x 43 cm/15 in x 17 in)
If you can't find cellophane in your local craft shop, buy some of the real thing from a florist instead.
Clear sticky tape
1 metre (39 in) yellow ribbon

fig 1

1 Shape the cake by slicing two long triangles off the sides and a slope into the front (*fig 1*). Place the cake diagonally onto the cake board.

2 Slice the cake in half and fill the centre with buttercream and then cover the top and sides with buttercream as well.

3 Knead and roll the white sugarpaste until it's about 3 mm (⅛ in) thick. Now carefully lift the icing and place over the cake, making sure that enough icing falls onto the board at the front of the cake for you to be able to make the folds later on.

4 Gather the icing up at the front and using a wooden spoon, coax the icing into folds (*fig 2*).

5 Wriggle your finger under the point at which the gathers meet the cake to make a tunnel through which you will thread

the ribbon later. Support the tunnel while it's drying by placing a bit of scrunched up clingfilm under the arch.

6 Trim and neaten the rest of the icing around the edges of the cake and secure the bits that rest on the board with a little water.

7 Make the leaves by rolling out about half of one of the green sugarpastes. Using a the tip of a sharp knife, cut out a simple leaf shape. Turn the knife over and press the back of it into the leaf to make a couple of simple veins. Place the leaf on a bit of partially crumpled tin foil so that it dries in a slightly irregular shape. Repeat with the other green sugarpastes, making a total of about fifty leaves in all.

8 To make the roses, take a 10 g (¼ oz) ball of yellow sugarpaste and roll it into a strip about 15 cm (6 in)

fig 2

long. Paint a line of water down the centre of the strip and roll it up (not too tightly) like a miniature Swiss roll. Tweak the rose into a point at the base and carefully bend back the top of the rose

fig 3

petals *(fig 3)*. Put a tiny ball of yellow sugarpaste to one side to make the iris centres later and use the rest to make a further eleven roses. Leave them to dry on their sides.

9 For the irises, take a pea-sized ball of violet sugarpaste and press it into a flat oval shape. Dab a little water in the centre and fold the icing almost in half. Bend the two ends back slightly and tweak the base into a point. Stick a tiny ball of yellow into the centre and place to dry on its side. Make another nine irises.

10 Place two tablespoons of green royal icing into a piping

bag fitted with a No 3 nozzle (round tip). Starting from just inside the folds at the front of the cake, pipe about eight flower stems.

11 Beginning from the top of the cake and working down, stick the roses and leaves into position with the royal icing.

12 Insert the irises into any gaps.

13 Tidy up any dusty icing sugar smudges with a damp paintbrush.

14 Place the cellophane over the cake. Secure the far end of the cellophane to the cake board with a couple of small

pieces of clear sticky tape. Gather the rest up at the front.

15 Thread the ribbon through the hole and tie a neat bow over the top of the cellophane.

16 Tweak the cellophane into place and secure at the sides with sticky tape.

TIP: *To give your bouquet that final touch, buy a card from a real florist complete with its own miniature envelope. Write your message and tuck it into the bow.*

Golf course

Poor old Mister Mole. He'd just found a nice ready-made hole and had settled down for a sleep in when a nasty white thing landed on his head! This cake is easier to put together than it looks. The cake can be as irregular as you like and the shrubbery can be used to hide any imperfections in the icing.

INGREDIENTS

23 cm (9 in) round cake
1 ½ quantities buttercream
(see page 19)
1 kg (2 lb 4 oz) green
sugarpaste (rolled fondant)
70 g (2 ¾ oz) black sugarpaste
(rolled fondant)
25 g (1 oz) dark grey
sugarpaste (rolled fondant)
100 g (4 oz) white sugarpaste
(rolled fondant)
100 g (4 oz) darker green
sugarpaste (rolled fondant)
Silver and black food colours
2 tsp light golden sugar
Icing (confectioners') sugar,
for rolling out
Water

UTENSILS

25 cm (10 in) square cake
board
Carving knife
Small sharp knife
Palette knife (metal spatula)
Rolling pin
Cake smoothers
Paintbrushes, one medium,
one fine
Ball tool or wooden spoon
Two cocktail sticks
(toothpicks), optional
Sieve (strainer)
Small plastic bags

fig 1

1 Slice the top off the cake to level it if necessary and place it upside down on the cake board. Carve away part of the sides of the cake so that it now forms a slightly irregular shape. Cut out a hole slightly towards the rear of the cake approximately 5 cm (2 in) wide and 2.5 cm (1 in) deep *(fig 1)*. Slice and fill the centre of the cake with buttercream. Reassemble the cake and spread a thin layer of buttercream around the sides and top.

2 Knead and roll out the of green sugarpaste to a thickness of about 1 cm (½ in). Carefully lift it and place over the cake. Smooth over the top and sides, first with your hands, then with a pair of smoothers. Don't worry if the icing tears when you're pushing it into the hole as this will be hidden by the mole's body later. Trim away the

excess icing (there should be about 300 g/11 oz). Store it in a plastic bag for making bushes later.

3 Now make the mole by rolling 50 g (2 oz) black sugarpaste into a ball and place this into the hole. Make a head by moulding the dark grey sugarpaste into a cone shape. Stick this onto the mole's body with a little water, making sure that the thinnest part of the cone is facing forwards.

Roll 10 g (¼ oz) white sugarpaste into a thin sausage approximately 15 cm (6 in) long. Lightly moisten the edge of the hole with a little water and lay the strip around the top edge and mole's body *(fig 2)*. Paint a disgruntled expression onto the mole's face using black food colour and a fine paintbrush.

Add two small tapering sausages of black sugarpaste

fig 2

for arms. Position one as though he is rubbing his eye and the other resting on the ground.

4 To make the golf ball, roll 50 g (2 oz) white sugarpaste into a ball. Using either a ball tool or the end of a wooden spoon handle, poke small dents around the outside of the ball. Stick the ball into position.

5 For the golf club, make the metal part of the golf club out of 40 g (1 ½ oz) white sugarpaste shaped into a sort of 'L' shape. Flatten and round the edges of the base part and press a few horizontal lines into the still soft sugarpaste using the back of a knife. Make a handle out of 10 g (¼ oz) black sugarpaste rolled into a sausage. Make a few diagonal indented lines across the handle and finish with a few small holes made with the end of a paintbrush (*fig 3*). Place the golf club into

fig 3

position on the cake and paint the white metal section with silver food colour.

6 Lightly moisten the exposed cake board with a little water. Press about 200 g (7 oz) of the remaining green sugarpaste

around the board, forming small undulating slopes. Trim the edges.

7 Partially mix together the remaining mid-green sugarpaste and the dark green sugarpaste. Pull off a small ball and push it through a sieve. Cut and lift the strands of sugarpaste away from the sieve with a sharp knife and place onto the cake, sticking into place with a little water. Continue around the sides of the cake hiding the joins and any blemishes in the icing as you go.

8 Moisten the bunker area with a little water. Carefully spoon about two teaspoons of light golden sugar onto the board. Brush away any stray bits of sugar with a dry paintbrush.

TIP: *If the golf ball won't stay in position on the mole's head, remove the ball and insert two cocktail sticks (toothpicks) into the mole's head, leaving about 2.5 cm (1 in) protruding. Then place the ball back in position. The cocktail sticks will provide additional support, but please ensure that nobody tries to eat the mole without removing them first.*

N.B. *Please note that the silver food colour is inedible and therefore the golf club should be discarded when cutting the cake.*

Christmas stocking

Just when everyone thinks that they've had all their surprises for the day, present this cake and wait for the gasps of admiration. If you have the time (usually in very short supply just before Christmas!) you could make small icing models for all the family and substitute them for the presents.

INGREDIENTS

15 cm (6 in) square fruit cake
900 g (2 lb) red sugarpaste
(rolled fondant)
275 g (10 oz) green sugarpaste
(rolled fondant)
500 g (1 lb 2 oz) white
sugarpaste (rolled fondant)
3 tbsp brandy
3 tbsp apricot jam
725 g (1 lb 10 oz) marzipan
26 edible gold balls
1 tsp red royal icing
(see page 20)
Icing (confectioners') sugar,
for rolling out
Water

UTENSILS

30 cm (12 in) gold-coloured
square cake board
Carving knife
Small sharp knife
Cocktail stick (toothpick)
Pastry brush
Rolling pin
Cake smoothers
Small holly cutter
Icing nozzle (tip)
Piping (decorating) bag fitted
with No 1 nozzle (round tip)
Small plastic bags for storing
icing

fig 1

1 Cut the cake in two so that one section measures 9 cm x 15 cm (3 ½ in x 6 in) and the other 7 cm x 15 cm (2 ½ in x 6 in). Place the thinner of the two strips at the base of the thicker one to produce the basic stocking shape *(fig 1)*. Cut small triangles away from the toe and heel of the stocking and also run a knife along the edges of the cake to make them rounded. Cut a slice about 2.5 cm (1 in) off the top of the cake to make the proportions look right and discard this piece.

2 Pierce the cake several times with a cocktail stick and drizzle the brandy over the cake. Allow the brandy to sink in, then place the cake onto the cake board.

3 Using a pastry brush, 'paint' the cake with warmed apricot jam.

4 Knead the marzipan on a surface dusted with icing sugar until it's nice and pliable. Roll it out into a rectangle approximately 5 mm (¼ in) thick and lift it over the cake. Ease it gently into position and trim away any excess marzipan. Run over the surface with cake smoothers.

5 Moisten the marzipan with a little water.

6 Knead and roll out 700 g (1 lb 8 oz) red sugarpaste. Lay this carefully over the marzipan. Trim away the excess and keep this for modelling the presents later. Neaten the top and sides of the stocking with cake smoothers.

fig 2

7 For the presents, you will need 200 g (7 oz) of red sugarpaste, 220 g (8 oz) of green sugarpaste and 100 g (4 oz) of white *(fig 2)*. Make two 50 g (2 oz) red squares for presents, a green and white ball, using about 50 g (2 oz) of both green and white. Then make a completely green 50 g (2 oz) ball.

For the candy canes, roll out two 25 g (1 oz) sausages of contrasting coloured icing. Twist the two sausages together and bend into a walking stick shape. Make three. Keep two back and pile the other one and the presents and balls up against the top of stocking, securing them with a little water.

8 Knead and roll 400 g (14 oz) white sugarpaste into a strip about 25 cm (10 in) long and about 13 cm (5 in) wide. Moisten the top of the stocking and lay the cuff into position so that it overlaps the presents slightly. Hold a piping nozzle at a slight angle and press it into the white to leave impressions in the still soft icing.

9 Slot the last two candy canes into position and secure with water.

10 Stick small flattened balls of white sugarpaste onto one of the red parcels to decorate it.

11 Thinly roll out 50 g (2 oz) green icing and cut out 26 holly leaves with a cutter.

Stick these onto the cake in pairs and press the back of a knife into each one three times to make veins *(fig 3)*.

12 Attach two gold balls beneath each pair of leaves using the red royal icing in the piping (decorating) bag and two tiny balls of red icing beneath the leaves on the cuff.

fig 3

TIP: *To take a lot of the hard work out of kneading marzipan, heat it in a microwave for a few seconds. However, don't overdo it or the oil in the centre will get very hot and could give you a nasty burn.*

Racing Car

I have a suspicion that this cake might appeal just as much to boys (and girls) of forty as those of four! If you don't have a loaf tin in which to bake your cake simply cut a square one to size instead.

1 Carve a tapering slope into the front of the cake. Round and neaten the top edges. Place into position diagonally across the cake board. Roll 30 g (1 oz) white sugarpaste into a pointed carrot shape and lay in front of the cake (1). Slice the cake horizontally and fill with a layer of buttercream. Reassemble then spread a thin layer of buttercream over the top and sides.

2 Dust your worksurface with icing sugar and knead 450 g (1 lb) yellow sugarpaste until soft and pliable. Roll it out and place over the car. Smooth the icing over the top and down the sides. If it starts to fall into pleats, lift and gently pull and fan the icing out. Slice about 3 cm (1 in) yellow sugarpaste off the point of the car to reveal the white sugarpaste "carrot" beneath. Moisten the "carrot" with a little water and keep the discarded yellow sugarpaste. Trim and neaten around the base.

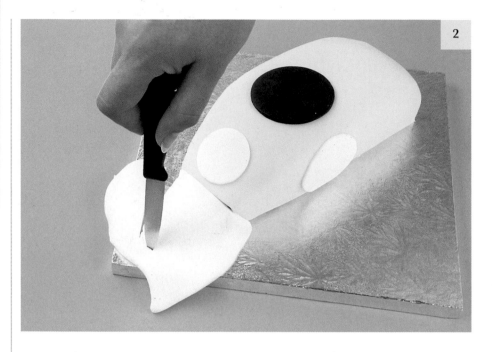

3 Roll out 30 g (1 oz) black sugarpaste and cut out a round, flat disc. Stick this on top of the car. Clean your fingers and roll out 30 g (1 oz) white sugarpaste. Using a circle cutter or a lid, cut out three discs. Stick one on the bonnet of the car and the other two on the sides. Knead the leftover white sugarpaste plus an additional 30 g (1 oz) together and roll out to the same thickness as the yellow sugarpaste that you used to cover the car. Slice a little off one edge and lay over the pointed front of the car (2). Butt the edge of the white right up against the edge of the yellow to make a neat seam and trim around the edges.

4 Roll 250 g (9 oz) white sugarpaste into a ball shape for the helmet. Stick this on the top black disc. Pull off and keep 20 g (¾ oz) red sugarpaste. Roll the rest into a thick, flattish conical shape and stick this behind the driver's head. Cut a thick rectangle out of 60 g (2 oz) black sugarpaste and stick this behind the red sugarpaste. Roll out 30 g (1 oz) yellow sugarpaste and cut out a slightly larger but thinner rectangle. Stick this on top of the black.

INGREDIENTS

- Cake baked in a 500 g (2lb) loaf tin (see page 15)
- 350 g (12 oz) white sugarpaste (rolled fondant)
- 1 quantity buttercream (see page 19)
- Icing (confectioners') sugar for rolling out
- 500 g (1 lb 2 oz) yellow sugarpaste (rolled fondant)
- 450 g (1 lb) black sugarpaste (rolled fondant)
- 150 g (5 oz) red sugarpaste (rolled fondant)
- 300 g (10½ oz) green sugarpaste (rolled fondant)
- 15 g (½ oz) flesh-coloured sugarpaste (rolled fondant)
- Black food colour paste
- 1 sheet rice paper
- 15 g (½ oz) green-coloured dessicated (shredded) coconut (optional, see page 20)

UTENSILS

- Carving knife
- 25 cm (10 in) square cake board
- Palette knife (metal spatula)
- Rolling pin
- Cake smoothers (optional)
- Small sharp knife
- Circle cutters or various sized lids
- Paintbrush
- Template for smoke (see page 141)
- Non-toxic pencil
- Scissors

5 Moisten the cake board around the car with a little water. Knead and thinly roll out 300 g (10 oz) green sugarpaste. Lay the sugarpaste in sections around the base of the cake (see page 22) until the board is hidden. Smooth into position, then trim and neaten the edges.

6 Make four thick 90 g (3 oz) black sugarpaste discs for the wheels and stick them into position around the car. Thinly roll out 30 g (1 oz) yellow sugarpaste and cut out four discs. Stick one in the centre of each wheel. Finish each one with a small flattened ball of red sugarpaste.

7 Roll out 5 g (⅛ oz) flesh-coloured sugarpaste and cut out a rectangle for the driver's face, seen through the helmet visor. Cut a tiny triangle off each corner to make a long, flat oval shape then stick it onto the front of the helmet, allowing it to curve slightly.

Paint the eyes on the flesh-coloured sugarpaste and the numbers on the car with black food colour. (See page 26 for hints about painting on sugarpaste.)

8 To make the tortoise, begin with the shell. Partially knead 30 g (1 oz) white sugarpaste and 5 g (⅛ oz) leftover green sugarpaste together to achieve a green marbled effect. Roll it into a ball, then pinch along the base to form a shell shape (3). Place to one side.

9 Roll 10 g (¼ oz) black sugarpaste into a sausage and cut in half for the wheels. Stand them side by side and stick the shell on top.

Decorate the wheels with tiny discs of white and red sugarpaste to match the racing car behind.

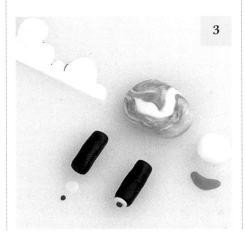

10 Stick a small ball of white sugarpaste on the front of the shell for his helmet and decorate with a very small flesh-coloured rectangle. Paint eyes on this and a few squares on the shell with the black food colour paste. Stick the tortoise on the board.

11 Draw a line of "smoke" (see template on page X) on a piece of rice paper and cut it out. Stick the "smoke" behind the tortoise, supporting it with balls of sugarpaste. To finish, you could sprinkle a few strands of coloured dessicated coconut around the board.

Handyman

Although this was designed with do-it-yourself fanatics in mind, this would make a good cake for someone who's just moved house and has all the joys of decorating ahead! Personalize the figure to resemble the recipient if you can.

■ INGREDIENTS

- 15 cm (6 in) square sponge cake
- 1 quantity buttercream (see page 19)
- Icing (confectioner's) sugar for rolling out
- 500 g (1 lb 2 oz) white sugarpaste (rolled fondant)
- 90 g (3 oz) blue sugarpaste (rolled fondant)
- 20 g (¾ oz) flesh-coloured sugarpaste (rolled fondant)
- Black food colour paste
- 30 g (1 oz) black sugarpaste (rolled fondant)
- 10 g (¼ oz) grey sugarpaste (rolled fondant)
- 110 g (3¾ oz) dark brown sugarpaste (rolled fondant)

■ UTENSILS

- Carving knife
- 20 cm (8 in) square cake board
- Palette knife (metal spatula)
- Small sharp knife
- Water and fine and medium paintbrushes
- Piping nozzle

1 Level the top of the cake, turn it upside down and place in the centre of the board. Slice the cake in half and fill the centre with buttercream. Reassemble the cake and spread a thin covering of buttercream around the top and sides.

2 Knead and roll out 400 g (14 oz) of white sugarpaste on a worksurface dusted with icing sugar. Carefully lay the icing over the cake. Smooth the icing into place and trim and neaten the base.

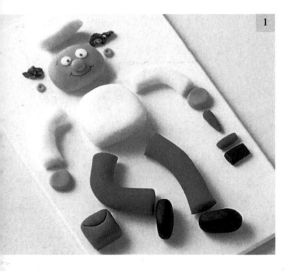

3 To construct the handyman himself, begin with the body. Roll 40 g (1¼ oz) of white sugarpaste into a cone (*fig 1*). Paint a little water in the middle of the cake and place his body in position. Next make his legs by rolling 40 g (1¼ oz) of blue sugarpaste into a sausage about 17 cm (7 in) long. Cut the sausage in half and bend the left leg slightly at the knee. Stick the legs in front of the body. For the arms, roll 20 g (¾ oz) of white sugarpaste into a thin sausage and cut it in half. Stick these either side of the handyman's body.

4 To make his head, use 10 g (¼ oz) of flesh-coloured sugarpaste and roll this into a ball. Slice a little icing off the top of his head to make a flat surface on which to attach the cap. Stick the head on top of the body. Flatten two tiny balls of white sugarpaste and stick these onto his face for his eyes. Add a tiny ball of flesh-coloured sugarpaste for his nose. Paint the pupils on the eyes and a smile on his face using black food colour and a fine paintbrush.

5 Partially mix a tiny amount of black sugarpaste with a little white for his hair. Scrunch and tear the icing into little bits and stick them to the sides of his head. Make a little cap by rolling 10 g (¼ oz) of white sugarpaste into a thick disc shape. Pinch and pull the icing on one side to form a peak. Stick this on his head. Finish off the head by sticking two tiny balls of flesh-coloured sugarpaste either side of the head for his ears. Add a little detail by making a small dent in each one with the end of a paintbrush.

6 Roll two 10 g (¼ oz) lumps of black sugarpaste into two oval shapes for his feet and stick one on the end of each leg.

7 To make the paint pot, roll 10 g (¼ oz) of grey sugarpaste into a stumpy cylindrical shape. Press an icing nozzle or something similar into the side to leave a semi-circular impression for the handle. Place the pot between his legs.

   For the paintbrush, make two tiny oblongs of brown sugarpaste and one of black. Stick them together like an upside-down 'T' shape and press lines into the black one with a knife to make bristles. Place the brush just in front of the handyman's left arm. Use two small flattened balls of flesh-coloured sugarpaste for his hands and stick these as though he is holding the paint pot and brush.

8 To make the planks of wood, roll 100 g (3½ oz) of dark brown sugarpaste and 20 g (¾ oz) of white together into a sausage.

Fold the sausage in half and roll again. Keep rolling and folding to achieve a woodgrain effect. Roll out the icing and cut out strips of varying lengths (*fig 2*). Stick a few on and around the cake.

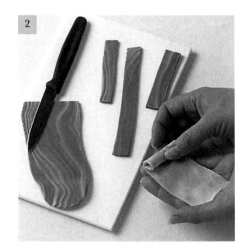

9 To make the rolls of wallpaper, partially knead 50 g (2 oz) of blue sugarpaste and 20 g (¾ oz) of white together to achieve a marbled effect. Carefully roll the sugarpaste out and cut out two strips. Roll one strip up completely and the other about halfway. Stick them onto the cake.

   Finally, dab splodges of black food colour around the cake and on the character himself.

Weary windsurfer

This cake was made for a keen windsurfing friend. If you don't feel up to painting, make the pool from one solid colour or stick spots or other sugarpaste shapes around the sides.

INGREDIENTS

- Icing (confectioners') sugar for rolling out
- 300 g (10½ oz) white sugarpaste (rolled fondant)
- 15 cm (6 in) round cake
- ½ quantity buttercream (see page 19)
- 30 ml (2 tbsp) royal icing (optional)
- 60 g (2 oz) orange sugarpaste (rolled fondant)
- 50 g (1¾ oz) flesh-coloured sugarpaste (rolled fondant)
- Assorted food paste colours for painting, including black and brown
- 60 g (2 oz) dark blue sugarpaste (rolled fondant)
- 1 candy stick (sweet cigarette)
- 30 g (1 oz) green-coloured sugar (see page 20)

UTENSILS

- Rolling pin
- Small sharp knife
- Surfboard template (see page 142)
- Carving knife
- Palette knife (metal spatula)
- Water
- Medium and fine paintbrushes
- Thin cardboard triangle for sail
- Clean damp cloth

1 Begin by making the surfboard. Roll out 40 g (1 ¾ oz) of white sugarpaste on a surface dusted with icing sugar and cut out a board shape, using the template if necessary. Place the board somewhere out of the way to harden slightly while you assemble the rest of the cake.

2 Level the top of the cake if necessary and turn it upside down. Slice and fill the middle of the cake with buttercream. Reassemble and place the cake in the centre of the cake board. Spread a thin layer of buttercream over the top and sides, saving some if using buttercream for the water.

3 Sprinkle the worksurface with icing sugar and roll out and cover the cake with the rest of the white sugarpaste. Smooth over the top and sides and trim away any excess from the base.

4 Begin constructing the windsurfer by building a life jacket. Shape the orange sugarpaste into a thick cone and press three vertical lines down the length of the jacket using the back of a knife (*fig 1*). Stick this onto the cake. Roll 20 g (¾ oz) of flesh-coloured sugarpaste into a ball for his head and stick in position. Paint in the eyes using black food colour and a fine paintbrush and stick three tiny balls of flesh-coloured sugarpaste on the face for his ears and nose. To add detail, poke the end of a paintbrush into each ear to leave a little hollow.

5 Take about half a teaspoon of royal icing or buttercream and mix in a little brown food colour. (A nice touch here would be to colour the hair the same shade as the recipient's.) Using a knife, smear the hair on top of the head and pull it up slightly to give it a bit of texture.

Roll 5 g (⅛ oz) of flesh-coloured sugarpaste into a sausage for one of the arms. Flatten one end slightly to make a hand and stick the arm against the side of the body, bending it at the elbow so that the hand covers the mouth area.

6 For the water, partially mix a little blue food colour into about 30 ml (2 tbsp) of royal icing or buttercream. Spread around the windsurfer on top of the cake (*fig 2*).

7 Roll the dark blue sugarpaste into a sausage about 46 cm (18 in) long. Starting from the back of the cake, lay this around the top edge. Neaten and stick the join together. Place the surfboard in position so that the tip just rests on the edge of the pool. Make two flattish oval shapes from flesh-coloured sugarpaste for his feet and insert these into the water. Make the other arm, squashing one end slightly to make a hand and stick this in place with the palm just resting on the board.

8 Cut a triangle out of thin cardboard and stick this to the candy stick with a little royal icing or buttercream. Insert this into the top of the cake.

9 Paint a design on the sides of the pool. Start by painting the colours first and add the outlines in black food colour afterwards. If you do it the other way round, the black will bleed into the colour. If you make a mistake, wash over the area with fresh water and wipe away the mistake with a clean, damp cloth.

10 Moisten the exposed cake board with a little water and carefully spoon the coloured sugar around the base to cover the rest of the board.

Enchanted house

You can make this cake as colourful as you like. Use whatever sweets (candies) take your fancy and if, after constructing the house, you find blemishes on the brickwork, use the sweets to hide them. If you can't get hold of 'hundreds and thousands' (rainbow nonpareils) for the path, use coloured sugar instead.

INGREDIENTS

2 x 15 cm (6 in) square sponges
2 quantities of buttercream (see page 19)
800 g (1 lb 12 oz) pink sugarpaste (rolled fondant)
50 g (2 oz) black sugarpaste (rolled fondant)
200 g (7 oz) white sugarpaste (rolled fondant)
50 g (2 oz) brown sugarpaste (rolled fondant)
10 g (¼ oz) grey sugarpaste (rolled fondant)
500 g (1 lb 2 oz) green sugarpaste (rolled fondant)
31 plain finger biscuits (cookies) (but have spares in case of breakages)
3 chocolate cream biscuits (cookies)
2 tbsp white royal icing (see page 20)
Edible gold balls
Assorted sweets, lollipops, candy canes
3 tsp 'hundreds and thousands' (rainbow nonpareils)
Water
Icing (confectioners') sugar, for rolling out on

UTENSILS

Utensils
30 cm (12 in) round cake board
Carving knife
Palette knife (metal spatula)
Rolling pin
Cake smoothers
Small sharp knife
Ruler
Piping (decorating) bag fitted with a No 3 (round) nozzle
Paintbrush

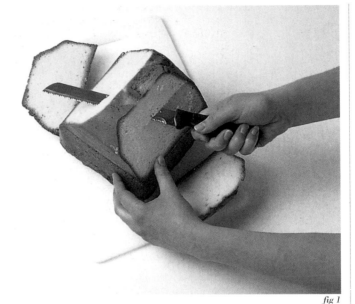

fig 1

1 Stack the two sponges on top of each other and cut the top one into a roof shape *(fig 1)*. Slice the cakes and fill the layers with buttercream. Spread buttercream around the top and sides.

2 Knead the pink sugarpaste on a surface dusted with icing sugar until it's pliable. Roll it out and place it over the cake. Smooth the sides, first with your hands and then with a pair of cake smoothers. Trim away any excess.

3 Make the brickwork by holding a ruler horizontally and pressing it into the icing while it's still soft *(fig 2)*. Press three lines into the sides of the house and six into the front and back. Press the back of a small knife vertically into the icing to pick out the individual bricks.

4 Split the chocolate cream biscuits in half to make the shutters. Roll the black icing out to a 3 mm (⅛ in) thickness.

Measure the height of the biscuits (cookies) and make the height of the windows slightly shorter. Cut out three windows with a width of 2.5 cm (1 in) Stick the black icing windows into position with a little water. Roll out 10 g (¼ oz) white sugarpaste and cut out six strips. Place two on each window in the shape of a cross. Trim to fit and secure into position with a little water. Using a little

royal icing stick half a chocolate cream biscuit each side of each window to make the shutters.

5 Roll out the brown sugarpaste and cut out a rectangle 5 cm x 2.5 cm (2 in x 1 in). Stick this to the front of the house to make a door and holding a knife vertically, press the back of it into the icing to make the wooden slats of the door.

6 Divide the grey sugarpaste into two slightly misshapen rectangles and stick these against the door, one on top of the other to make the steps.

7 For the roof, break 25 finger biscuits in half. Starting at the bottom of one slope, make a line of five half biscuits, securing them with dabs of royal icing. Now add another line of biscuits above these and repeat a further three times. Do this again on the other side *(fig 3)*. Lay five whole biscuits across the top of the roof.

8 Make a small chimney out of either a sweet (candy) or a small white and pink icing

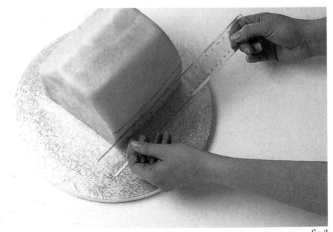

fig 2

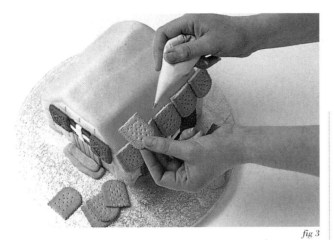

fig 3

'sandwich' and position with royal icing. Stick a line of pink sweets along the top of the roof to decorate.

9 Decorate the shutters with sweets securing them with a little royal icing.

10 Pipe a line of royal icing above the door and press a finger biscuit into this to make the porch. Stick an edible gold ball in place for a door handle.

11 Pipe dots along the top and bottom of the windows.

12 Stick two 65 g (2 ½ oz) and one 50 g (2 oz) lumps of white sugarpaste onto the cake board with a little water.

13 Knead and roll out the green sugarpaste. Moisten the white 'lumps' and the exposed cake board.

Lay the green around the house in sections (see page 22). Trim the edges of the board and cut and lift away a section at the front of the house to make a path.

14 Moisten the path with a little water and sprinkle with 'hundreds and thousands'. Edge the sides of the path with small sweets inserted into the icing. Stick a few sweets to the side of the house and around the garden and secure with royal icing if necessary. Insert a couple of candy canes and lollipops into the green lumps.

TIP: *Score a thin line across the middle of each finger biscuit with a sharp knife before breaking them in half.*

Football fan

Although the theme of this cake is football, it could be adapted to suit other sports. Substitute a brown sugarpaste oval and you have a rugby cake. Dress him in white with a bat and it becomes a cricket cake.

■ INGREDIENTS

- 5 cm (6 in) square sponge cake
- 1 quantity buttercream (see page 19)
- Icing (confectioners)' sugar for rolling out
- 350 g (12 oz) green sugarpaste (rolled fondant)
- 300 g (10½ oz) white sugarpaste (rolled fondant)
- 150 g (5 oz) red sugarpaste (rolled fondant)
- 20 g (¾ oz) black sugarpaste (rolled fondant)
- 30 g (1 oz) flesh-coloured sugarpaste (rolled fondant)
- 40 g (1¾ oz) blue sugarpaste (rolled fondant)
- Black food coloring
- 5 g (⅛ oz) brown sugarpaste (rolled fondant)
- 60 g (2 oz) green-coloured coconut (see page 19)

■ UTENSILS

- Carving knife
- 25 cm (10 in) square cake board
- Palette knife (metal spatula)
- Cake smoother (optional)
- Small sharp knife
- Water
- Medium and fine paintbrushes

1 Slice a little off the top of the cake to level it if necessary. Turn it upside down and place toward the back of the board. Slice and fill the middle of the cake with buttercream, then reassemble and spread a thin covering of butter cream over the top and sides.

2 Dust the work surface with a little icing sugar and knead all the green sugarpaste until pliable. Roll it out, then lift and place over the cake. Smooth over the top and sides, preferably with a cake smoother, as this irons out any lumps and bumps. Alternatively, simply smooth it as best you can with the flat of your hand. Trim away any excess from around the base.

3 Make the scarf by rolling out 250 g (8 oz) of the white sugarpaste and cutting it into a strip 30 cm x 10 cm (12 in x 4 in). Moisten the top of the cake and carefully lay the scarf over the top.

Roll out and cut 150 g (5 oz) of red sugarpaste into about seven thin strips about 3 cm x 10 cm (11 in x 4 in). Lay and stick the red stripes across the scarf. When you come to the ones at either end, cut a fringe into the strip before laying it into position on the board *(fig 1)*.

4 Begin with the footballer's feet. Divide the black sugarpaste in two and roll each half into an oval. Stick these onto the board in front of the cake. Make two socks by rolling

10 g (¼ oz) white sugarpaste into two balls. Flatten each ball slightly and press a few horizontal lines into each sock with the back of a knife. Stick these onto the boots *(fig 2)*.

Make the footballer's legs by rolling 10 g (¼ oz) flesh-coloured sugarpaste into a thin string. Cut this in half and stick into position.

5 For his shorts, take 10 g (¼ oz) white sugarpaste and roll it into a boomerang shape *(fig 3)*. Stick on top of the cake. Pull off and keep a little bit of the blue ready-to-roll fondant to make the sleeves later. Roll the rest into a cone for his body and stick

TIP

If the footballer loses his head or falls over, insert a small strand of dried spaghetti inside the body and slot the head on top for extra support.

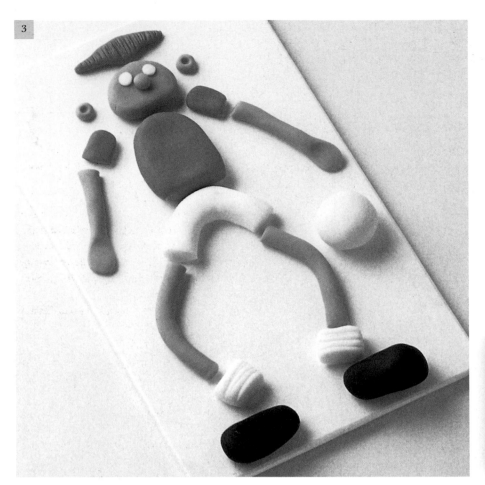

3

making a small dent in them with the end of a paintbrush.

Paint in the pupils, eyebrows and mouth with black food colouring. Finally, roll a little brown sugarpaste into a tiny strip and place on top of the head. Press some lines into the hair with the back of a knife.

9 Moisten the top of the cake and any exposed cake board with a little water and then sprinkle with the green-coloured coconut to look like the grass of a football pitch.

TIP

If you know the home colours of the recipient's favourite team, make the scarf and the footballer's kit in the appropriate shades.

on top of the shorts *(fig 3)*. Flatten the top of the cone slightly so the head has a level surface to sit on.

6 For the ball, roll 20 g (¾ oz) white sugarpaste into a ball. Stick this in place and paint a hexagonal design on the front with black food colouring and a fine paintbrush. (If you don't want to paint, just press a few lines into the ball with the back of a knife or leave it plain.)

7 Roll 5 g (⅛ oz) flesh-coloured sugarpaste into a thin sausage to make his arms. Cut in two and flatten one end of each half to make the hands. Stick these into position.

Make two tiny shirt sleeves by rolling the leftover blue sugarpaste into an oval. Cut in half and stick one on the top of each arm.

8 To make the head, roll 10 g (¼ oz) flesh-coloured sugarpaste into a ball. Stick on top of the body.

Stick two tiny flattened disks of white sugarpaste onto the face for his eyes and three small balls of flesh-coloured sugarpaste in position for his ears and nose. Add some detail to the ears by

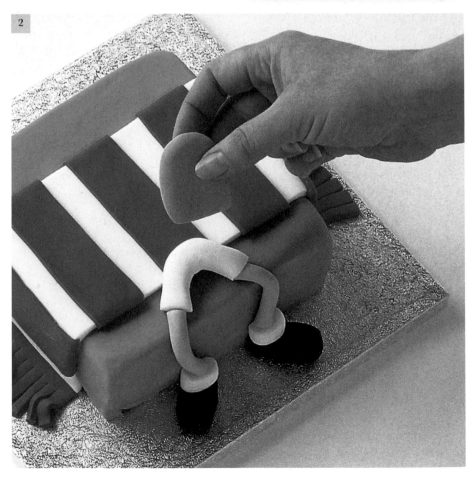

2

Comfy Chair

Unless they have a hobby, men can be difficult subjects to make cakes for. This is a neat solution, ideal for a birthday or Father's Day. If it's children that harangue him rather than a cat, substitute a child climbing over the back instead.

1 Cover the board with white sugarpaste as on page 21. Trim off excess and put the board to one side *(fig 1)*.

2 Cut the cake into shape by slicing off about one third. Place the smaller, cutaway piece flat side down on the remaining section of cake to form the basic seat shape *(fig 2)*. If there is not much seat area, slice a thin section away from the back of the chair. "Glue" the two sections of seat together with butter cream. Spread a layer of buttercream over the outside of the cake.

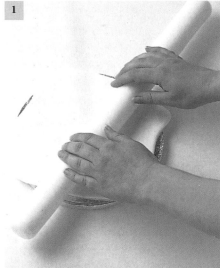

3 Knead and roll out 300 g (10½ oz) pale blue sugarpaste. Carefully lift up the icing and place over the cake. To prevent air being trapped, start from the central seat area and smooth the icing into position. You may find that icing gathers into folds at the back of the chair. These can usually be eased out by gently lifting and fanning the icing out slightly. Trim and neaten the base.

4 Carefully lift and place the cake toward the back of the covered cake board. If you're worried about getting fingerprints in the icing, use a fish slice to lift it.

5 Roll out about 50 g (2 oz) of the pale blue sugarpaste. Cut out a strip about 46 cm x 3 cm (18 in x 1¼ in). Ideally the strip should be slightly wavy down one of the longest sides. This is not essential but it does make for a better frill. Making sure you have plenty of icing sugar on the work surface to prevent the frill from sticking, roll a paintbrush or cocktail stick backward and forward over the wavy edge of the strip *(fig 3)*. Paint a line of water around the side of the cake, about 3 cm (¼ in) up from the base. Stick the frill around the cake. Neaten the join by pushing the end of a paintbrush along the top of the strip to leave a circular pattern.

6 To make the cushions, roll out about 60 g (2 oz) white sugarpaste fairly thickly. Cut out three squares about 6 cm (2½ in) square. Tweak the ends slightly and using the end of a drinking straw, poke four small circles into each one to look like buttons *(fig 4)*. Stick the cushions onto the back of the chair.

INGREDIENTS

- Icing (confectioners') sugar for rolling out
- 160 g (5½ oz) white sugarpaste (rolled fondant)
- 15 cm (6 in) round sponge cake
- ½ quantity buttercream (see page 19)
- 350 g (12½ oz) pale blue sugarpaste (rolled fondant)
- 80 g (2¾ oz) grey sugarpaste (rolled fondant)
- 20 g (¾ oz) black sugarpaste (rolled fondant)
- 80 g (2¾ oz) green sugarpaste (rolled fondant)
- 30 g (1 oz) flesh-coloured sugarpaste (rolled fondant)
- Black food colouring
- 10 g (1¼ oz) brown sugarpaste (rolled fondant)

UTENSILS

- 20 cm (8 in) round cake board
- Water and paintbrush
- Rolling pin
- Small sharp knife
- Carving knife
- Fish slice (pancake turner)
- Palette knife (metal spatula)
- Cocktail stick (toothpick) (optional)
- Drinking straw

7 To make the man himself, begin with his legs. Roll 80 g (2¾ oz) grey sugarpaste into a long sausage. Cut the sausage in half and stick it onto the chair. Roll two 10 g (¼ oz) lumps of black sugarpaste into oval shapes for his feet and stick one on the end of each leg.

Decorating variation

A comfy chair is not just for people to snooze in — in fact, once you have made the basic shape you could sit virtually anything on it. The cat in this variation looks especially at home! Make a potato like those in the flowerpot cake (page 114) decorate it with eyes and a mouth, sit it on the seat, and you have an cheeky couch-potato cake. A chair cake is an extremely useful shape to add to your repertoire because it provides an easy way to put full-length, upright figures onto a cake without having to fiddle about with awkward supports inside them.

10 To make the newspaper, cut a flat rectangle out of 10 g (¼ oz) white sugarpaste. Fold the icing in half, then half again. Paint squiggles onto the newspaper with black food colouring to resemble the print and stick the paper onto the man's lap.

11 To make the cat, roll about 5 g (⅛ oz) brown sugarpaste into a tapering sausage shape for his body. Pinch a couple of small ears out of the thicker end.

Stick two tiny strings of brown sugarpaste onto the back of the chair for his paws and stick the body on top. Roll another tiny piece of icing into a string for his tail. Paint on the cat's features and stripes neatly with some black food colouring.

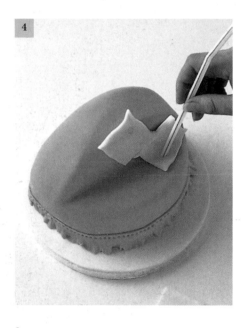

as I did, that the head flops backwards, simply prop it up with a small triangle of white sugarpaste which will just look like another cushion. Push the end of a paintbrush into the lower part of the head and pull it down slightly to give him an open-mouthed expression.

Stick a small ball of fondant on the front of the face for his nose and two at the sides for his ears. Add a little detail to the ears by making a small hollow with the end of a paintbrush. Either paint in the eyes with black food colouring or press two semi-circular impressions into the face using the drinking straw held at an angle.

Add two flattened balls of flesh-coloured sugarpaste for his hands.

8 Make his body by rolling 50 g (2 oz) green sugarpaste into a conical shape and stick this on top of the legs (*fig 5*). Roll out a thin strip of the same colour green and press vertical lines into the strip using the back of your knife. Lay this around the base of his jumper. Make a polo neck by sticking a small but thick disk of green sugarpaste on top of the jumper and again press a few vertical lines around the edge.

For his arms, roll 20 g (¾ oz) of the green sugarpaste into a sausage. Cut it in half and arrange and stick the arms in whatever position you wish.

9 To make the man's head, roll 20 g (¾ oz) flesh-coloured sugarpaste into a ball (*fig 6*). Stick this onto the neck. If you find,

To make the golden brown colour for the puppy, either knead some orange or brown sugarpaste together or colour some white sugarpaste using "autumn leaf" food colour paste. Alternatively, you might be able to buy a ready-coloured sugarpaste called "teddy bear brown" from your local cake decorating shop. Or you could make him a different colour completely!

1 Moisten the cake board with a little water and cover using the pale blue sugarpaste (see page 19 for details.) Place the covered board to one side.

2 Level the top of the cake if it's very rounded. Slice horizontally and fill with buttercream. Reassemble the cake and spread a thin covering of butter-cream over the top and sides. Cover and keep the leftover buttercream. Lift up the cake using a fish slice so you don't get your fingers all sticky and place it slightly towards the rear of the board.

3 For the dog basket, roll 100 g (3½ oz) dark brown sugarpaste into a sausage about 50 cm (20 in) long. Cut into four equal lengths and stick them on top of each other on the right hand side of the cake (1).

Press diagonal lines going in alternative directions into each of the strands. Repeat with another four strands on the other side of the cake.

4 To make the puppy's slipper, roll two 60 g (2 oz) lumps of red sugarpaste into flat, chunky oval shapes and cut one in half. Scrunch up one of the halves and stick on one end of the other oval (2). Place the remaining half over the top of the scrunched oval to form the foot of the slipper.

Using either a section of a jam tart cutter or a large drinking straw, cut a "bite" out of the heel. Stick the slipper slightly towards the left of the front of the cake.

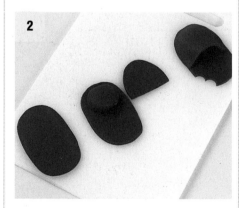

5 To make the puppy's head, roll 200 g (7 oz) golden brown sugarpaste into a thick oval. Flatten one end slightly to form the dog's forehead (3). Bend this thinner end up at a right angle and stick against the cake allowing the muzzle to rest on the cake board.

Press a short vertical line into the front of the dog's face using the back of a knife to make his mouth and poke three small hollows into his muzzle with the end of a paintbrush.

6 Roll two 30 g (1 oz) pieces of golden brown sugarpaste into tapering carrot shapes then flatten them slightly to make his paws. Stick one resting possessively on the slipper (most of this will be hidden by his ear later) and the other just touching his muzzle. Press three lines into the end of each paw with the back of a knife.

INGREDIENTS

- Icing (confectioner's) sugar for rolling out
- 300 g (10 oz) pale blue sugarpaste (rolled fondant)
- 18 cm (7 in) round sponge cake (see page 14)
- 1 quantity buttercream (see page 19)
- 250 g (9 oz) dark brown sugarpaste (rolled fondant)
- 150 g (5 oz) red sugarpaste (rolled fondant)
- 350 g (12 oz) golden brown sugarpaste (rolled fondant)
- 550 g (1 lb 3 oz) white sugarpaste (rolled fondant)
- 30 g (1 oz) black sugarpaste (rolled fondant)
- Black and brown food colour pastes
- 15 g (½ oz) yellow sugarpaste (rolled fondant)
- 15 g (½ oz) green sugarpaste (rolled fondant)
- 15 g (½ oz) dark blue sugarpaste (rolled fondant)

EQUIPMENT

- 30 cm (12 in) round cake board
- Rolling pin
- Carving knife
- Palette knife (metal spatula)
- Fish slice (pancake turner) (optional)
- Small sharp knife
- Jam tart cutter or drinking straw
- Paintbrush
- Fork

7 For the eyes, cut two small round discs out of about 15 g (½ oz) white sugarpaste and pull them slightly to form ovals. Stick them onto the dog's face. Add two smaller black ovals for the pupils and two tiny white sugarpaste dots for highlights.

Roll 10 g (¼ oz) golden brown sugarpaste into a ball and flatten into a disc. Cut the disc in half to make his eyelids. Stick one half over each eye at an angle.

8 To make his nose, roll about 5 g (⅛ oz) black sugarpaste into an oval. Stick onto the muzzle and top with a tiny round, white sugarpaste highlight.

For the ears, make two 30 g (1 oz) golden brown sugarpaste ovals. Flatten the two ovals slightly and stick against the head allowing them to flop over the eyes and paws. Colour the remaining buttercream brown and carefully spread onto the ears. "Rough up" the buttercream with a fork to give them a hairy effect.

Carol suggests

You can leave the ears plain if you prefer or if you want to save a bit of time.

9 Stick two 20 g (¾ oz) lumps of white sugarpaste on top of the cake to form the bumps under the blanket and moisten them with a little water.

To make the blanket, roll out 450 g (1 lb) white sugarpaste to about 15 cm (6 in) square. Break and roll about 15 g (½ oz) each of yellow, green, red and dark blue sugarpaste into small balls and place onto the white. Continue to roll out the icing to about 23 cm (9 in) square, pressing the coloured balls into the white as you go (4). Slice a little off all four edges to neaten them. Cut a fringe into two opposite sides. Carefully lay the blanket so that it covers all the exposed cake but leaves the dogs face and some of the wicker basket showing.

10 To make the dog biscuits, make two 15 g (½ oz) dark brown sugarpaste sausages and press and flatten both ends of each sausage. Using the end of a paintbrush, push the icing in slightly at either end of the biscuit to form a bone shape. Press a line of dots down the centre of the bone with the end of a paintbrush and stick them on the board around the puppy.

To finish, paint a few lines on the slipper with black food colour.

Candles

Insert the candles into sugarpaste balls and stick around the outside edge of the board, away from the sides of the cake.

Christmas crackers

This novel way of decorating an ordinary square fruit cake should tempt even the most turkey-stuffed palate on Christmas afternoon. You could decorate the board with small gifts appropriate to your guests or arrange real crackers around them to make a stunning centrepiece for the Christmas table.

INGREDIENTS

18 cm (7 in) square fruit cake
150 g (5 oz) black sugarpaste
(rolled fondant)
400 g (14 oz) red sugarpaste
(rolled fondant)
400 g (14 oz) green sugarpaste
(rolled fondant)
4 tbsp brandy
3 tbsp apricot jam
1 kg (2 lb 4 oz) marzipan
1 tbsp white royal icing (see
page 20)
Icing (confectioners') sugar,
for rolling out
Water

UTENSILS

30 cm (12 in) gold-coloured
square cake board
Carving knife
Small sharp knife
Cocktail stick (toothpick)
Pastry brush
Rolling pin
Cake smoothers
Clingfilm (plastic wrap)
Paintbrush
No 3 piping nozzle (round tip)
Piping (decorating) bag fitted
with No 1 nozzle (round tip)
2 m (2 yards 7 in) tartan
ribbon
Fish slice (pancake turner)

fig 1

fig 2

7 Moisten the ends of the cracker with water. Roll out 200 g (7 oz) red sugarpaste and cut out two strips about 20 cm x 7.5 cm (8 in x 3 in) Serrate one edge and wind around one end of the cracker (*fig 2*). Press the back of a knife into the icing a few times to make creases and tweak the jagged edges so that they stand out slightly. If they keep flopping, support them with a ball of scrunched up clingfilm until they dry.

1 Cut the cake into two 5 cm (2 in) strips. Use the remaining cake to extend the length of the first two strips (*fig 1*). Run a knife along the two long edges of each cracker to slightly round them.

2 Pierce both cakes a few times using a cocktail stick and pour the brandy over the holes.

3 Cover both crackers with a pastry brush dipped into warmed apricot jam.

4 Dust your work surface with a little icing sugar and knead 500 g (1 lb 2 oz) marzipan until pliable.

Smooth down the marzipan using your hands and a pair of cake smoothers and trim away any excess. Press a finger round the cracker to make a dent about 5 cm (2 in) from one end. Repeat at the other end. (This 'dent' is visible in *fig 2*.)

5 Repeat the above steps on the second cracker.

6 Measure the ends of the crackers and moisten with a little water. Roll out the black sugarpaste. Cut out four circles slightly larger than the ends of the crackers. Stick one circle onto each end.

8 Roll out 200 g (7 oz) of green sugarpaste. Cut out a strip 20 cm x 13 cm (8 in x 5 in). Moisten the centre of the cracker and wind the strip around it. Take a No 3 piping nozzle and press a line of decorative circles along both edges of the strip.

9 Repeat the above procedures on the second cracker, except this time use green sugarpaste for the ends of the cracker and red for the central strip.

10 Pipe small loops along the edges of the central strips using a No 1 nozzle and white royal icing (*fig 3*).

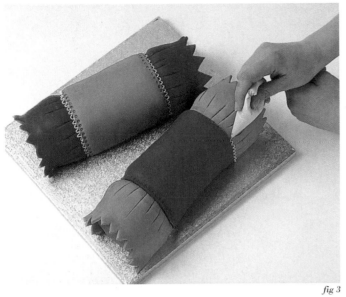

11 Pipe a line of small dots around the jagged edges of both crackers.

12 Lift and arrange both crackers on the board using a fish slice (pancake turner).

13 Cut two strips of tartan ribbon approximately 23 cm (9 in) long. Place one diagonally across the central strip of each cracker and secure with a little royal icing.

14 Finally, make two neat bows and stick on the top of each cracker with a little blob of royal icing.

TIP: *If you don't fancy piping around the centres of the crackers, drape some tinsel over the edges instead for a sparkling alternative look. Remove the tinsel before eating.*

fig 3

Lovebirds

Here's a novel idea for an engagement cake without a pink sugar heart in sight! It would also make a loving gift for Valentine's day. This is an extremely easy cake to put together as the chocolate sticks hide a multitude of sins!

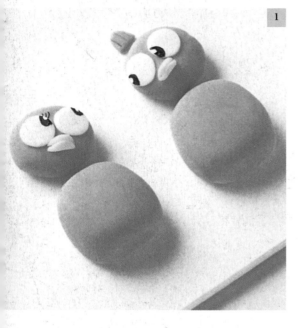

INGREDIENTS

- Icing (confectioners') sugar for rolling out
- 120 g (4 oz) pale blue sugarpaste (rolled fondant)
- 10 g (¼ oz) white sugarpaste (rolled fondant)
- Black food colouring
- 1 pudding bowl cake (see page 19)
- ½ quantity chocolate buttercream (see page 19)
- Two 120 g (4 oz) boxes of chocolate sticks (flavour of your choice!)
- 60 g (2 oz) dark blue sugarpaste (rolled fondant)
- 30 g (1 oz) green sugarpaste (rolled fondant)

UTENSILS

- Water
- Fine and medium paintbrushes
- Rolling pin
- Piping nozzle
- Small sharp knife
- Carving knife
- 8-in round cake board
- Palette knife (metal spatula)
- Template for tail (see page 142)
- Garrett frill or jam tart cutter

1. Roll two 60 g (2 oz) lumps of pale blue sugarpaste into two conical shapes for the birds' bodies. Check that the bases are flat enough for them to stand upright. Make two 30 g (1 oz) balls of pale blue sugarpaste for the heads (*fig 1*). Stick a head onto each body with a little water.

2. To make the eyes, thinly roll out about 10 g ¼ oz white sugarpaste. Cut out four small circles using a piping nozzle and stick two on each head. Paint pupils and eyelashes using black food colouring. Make two tiny yellow sugarpaste triangles for the beaks. Press a line using the back of a knife into the sides of each beak and stick one on each bird. Make a tiny pale blue triangle and press a few lines into the front of it. Stick it on top of the male bird's head. Put the birds to one side.

3. Level the top of the cake if necessary and slice and fill the centre with buttercream. Reassemble the cake and dab a little buttercream in the centre of the cake board to help hold the cake in place. Stand the cake, widest part up, and spread a thick layer of buttercream all over the sides and top.

4. Place the two birds into position on top of the cake and begin to build up the nest. Do this by pressing the chocolate sticks, one at a time, around the sides of the nest (*fig 2*) and over the top edge.

5. Roll out 30 g (1 oz) of the dark blue sugarpaste and cut out a tail using the template on page 142 if necessary. Re-knead the leftover icing and cut out a second tail. Place the two tails in position, one behind each bird.

6. To make the birds' wings, roll out another 30 g (1 oz) dark blue sugarpaste and using either a garrett frill or a jam tart cutter, cut out a frilly circle. Re-knead the sugarpaste and cut out a second circle of the same size. Cut both circles in half. Carefully stick two wings onto each of the birds, overlapping them slightly at the front as though they are holding hands (sorry – wings!) (*fig 3*).

7. Roll out the green sugarpaste and cut out some simple leaves. Press a couple of veins into each leaf using the back of a knife and stick the leaves around the board and against the cake with a little water.

Space Age

A great cake for any child (or adult) with star gazing tendencies. To give the moon an authentic gravelly look, I covered the cake using marzipan. However, if you don't like marzipan, you could use cream-coloured sugarpaste instead.

1 Carve the edges of the cake into an even dome shape. Slice and fill the cake with buttercream and spread a thin covering around the top and sides. Place two 15 g (½ oz) lumps of white marzipan on top of the cake to form the three-dimensional craters. Knead the rest of the marzipan until pliable. Roll it out and place over the cake. Smooth the surface of the marzipan and trim away any excess from the base of the cake. Place the cake onto the centre of the cake board.

2 Using items with a smooth, rounded end, such as a ball tool or a wooden spoon handle, carefully poke various sized hollows over the surface of the cake to form craters and also make holes in the centre of the two raised craters (1). Try not to break through into the cake beneath. If you do, patch any mistakes with marzipan. Press lines into the sides of the raised craters with the back of a knife.

Use some of the marzipan offcuts to roll moon rocks to place around the top of the cake. (These are also useful for covering any cracks in or blemishes on the marzipan.)

Roll out the dark blue sugarpaste and cover the cake board around the cake using the bandage method of covering (see page 22).

Carol suggests

Don't spread the buttercream too thickly between the layers as there will be a lot of weight on top of the cake and you don't want it breaking through the marzipan.

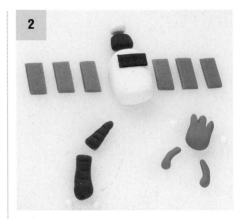

3 To make the green alien (2), first drape two tiny sausage shapes of green sugarpaste over the edge of the rear crater for the alien's arms. Next, roll the remaining green sugarpaste into an oval. Make three cuts in the top and splay slightly.

Stick two tiny discs of white sugarpaste onto the front for his eyes and place the alien's head in the crater.

INGREDIENTS
- 18 cm (7 in) round sponge cake (see page 14)
- 1 quantity buttercream (see page 19)
- 600 g (1 lb 5 oz) white marzipan
- Icing (confectioners') sugar for rolling out
- 150 g (5 oz) dark blue sugarpaste (rolled fondant)
- 15 g (½ oz) green sugarpaste (rolled fondant)
- 350 g (12 oz) white sugarpaste (rolled fondant)
- 30 g (1 oz) red sugarpaste (rolled fondant)
- Black, edible gold and yellow food colour paste
- 1 strand raw, dried spaghetti (optional)
- 90 g (3 oz) grey sugarpaste (rolled fondant)
- 30 g (1 oz) black sugarpaste (rolled fondant)
- 10 g (¼ oz) flesh-coloured sugarpaste (rolled fondant)

EQUIPMENT
- Carving knife
- Palette knife (metal spatula)
- Rolling pin
- Small sharp knife
- 25 cm (10 in) round cake board
- Ball tool or wooden spoon
- Paintbrush

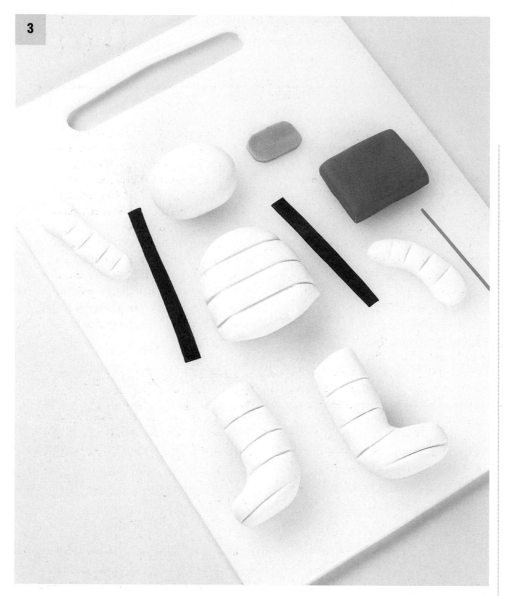

7 Roll 50 g (2 oz) white sugarpaste into an oval for his head and stick onto the body. Roll about 15 g (½ oz) white sugarpaste into a sausage for an arm and stick onto the body. Press lines into the arm as before. Repeat for the other arm. Roll out the flesh-coloured sugarpaste and cut out a rectangle. Cut a tiny triangle off each corner to turn it into an oval shape and stick it onto the front of the spaceman's helmet. Using black food colouring, paint a happy expression on his face.

8 To make the spaceship, roll 60 g (2 oz) of white sugarpaste into a conical shape. Stick a tapering disc of red sugarpaste on top of the cone and top with a small white pointed piece. Press a few lines into the red band. Roll out about 30 g (1 oz) grey sugarpaste and cut out about six small grey rectangles. Place the spaceship into position on the cake and stick the grey rectangles vertically around the ship's base. Stick a small black rectangle onto the front of the ship.

Carol suggests

Instead of painting stars around the cake, you could cut out small sugarpaste star and moon shapes. Alternatively, you could use paper ones – but be sure that nobody eats them!

9 Finally, wipe over the blue border using a damp paint- or pastry brush to remove any icing sugar marks. When it has dried, paint little moons and stars scattered around the base using edible gold or yellow food colour. Highlight the craters by painting them with a little watered-down yellow food colour.

Candles

Make thick sugarpaste or marzipan stars, discs or balls for candleholders, and stick around the outside of the cake board.

4 For the worm (2), roll two-thirds of the red sugarpaste into a sausage. Bend one end over slightly to make a head and press a few lines into his back with the back of a knife. Place him into the second crater. Stick two tiny white sugarpaste discs on his face for eyes. Make his mouth by poking the end of a paintbrush into the lower part of his head, pulling downwards slightly. Roll a little more red sugarpaste into a smaller tapering sausage shape and stick this onto the cake as though poking out of a nearby crater. Paint pupils on the eyes of both creatures using black food colour.

5 To make the spaceman (3), roll 90 g (3 oz) white sugarpaste into a conical shape for the body. Press lines back and front with the back of a knife. Stick in position on the cake.

For the legs, take 100 g (3½ oz) white sugarpaste. Cut in two and roll each half into a sausage. Bend one end of each leg up slightly to form a foot and stick the legs into position on the cake. Press lines into the legs as before.

Carol suggests

For extra security for the spaceman's body, stick a strand of raw, dried spaghetti into his torso. Leave a little protruding on which to slot the head.

6 To make the power pack, take 60 g (2 oz) grey coloured sugarpaste and form a rectangle. Stick it on the spaceman's back. Roll out a little black sugarpaste and cut out two thin straps. Stick these across the front of the body.

Doll

Make your cake designs sit up and take notice with the aid of two pudding bowl cakes. As a tasty alternative to sponge, you could substitute with the chocolate chip cakes as described on page 15.

1 Take the two cakes and slice a little off the base of one cake so that it sits comfortably on the board and won't fall over. Turn the second cake onto its side and slice away a strip of cake from the base so that it sits securely on top of the first cake (1).

If the top of the base cake is too rounded and the head falls off, slice a little off the top of the first cake to flatten it. Carve away any unsightly corners on the second cake to make a rounded head shape. Remove the head cake and place to one side.

2 Slice and fill the base cake horizontally with one or two layers of buttercream. Don't overdo it though – the body will have to support a lot of weight and if you sandwich it using too much buttercream, it will simply squish out of the sides of the cake. If you are using a chocolate chip cake as a base then you won't need to fill with buttercream – it should be rich enough without a filling. Place the base cake towards the rear of the cake board.

3 Spread a thin layer of buttercream over the outside of the cake. Knead and roll out 400 g (14 oz) of pink sugarpaste. Place over the cake and smooth into position. Trim away any excess from around the base and place the cake and board to one side. Buttercream and cover the head with 300 g (10½ oz) flesh-coloured sugarpaste. Trim and neaten the icing around the base.

4 For added security to stop the head from falling off the body, you could push a plastic cake dowel through the middle of the base cake. It should go right down until it reaches the cake board, leaving about 5–8 cm (2–3 in) protruding from the top. Place the head into position (2).

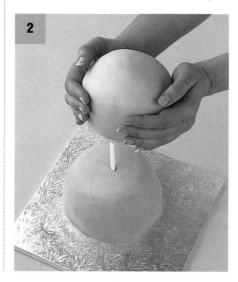

5 For the eyes, roll out 30 g (1 oz) white sugarpaste and cut out two discs using a circle cutter or lid. Pull each of the circles to stretch it into an oval shape and stick onto the face. Stick a small ball of flesh-coloured sugarpaste underneath for her nose.

Paint her eyeballs, eyelashes and mouth using black food colour and a paintbrush (see page 26 for hints about painting on sugarpaste). Also paint a few freckles around her nose and two discs on her cheeks with red food colour paste.

Carol suggests

Remember that you can use decorative features, such as the collar and mobcap, to hide any problem areas.

INGREDIENTS

- 2 pudding bowl cakes (see page 15)
- 1 quantity buttercream (see page 19)
- Icing (confectioner's) sugar for rolling out
- 450 g (1 lb) pink sugarpaste (rolled fondant)
- 450 g (1 lb) flesh-coloured sugarpaste* (rolled fondant)
- 560 g (1 lb 4 oz) white sugarpaste (rolled fondant)
- Black and red food colour pastes
- 300 g (10½ oz) pale blue sugarpaste (rolled fondant)
- 200 g (7 oz) yellow sugarpaste (rolled fondant)

EQUIPMENT

- Carving knife
- Palette knife (metal spatula)
- 25 cm (10 in) square cake board
- Rolling pin
- Small sharp knife
- Cake smoothers (optional)
- Plastic cake dowel (available from cake decorating shops)
- Assorted circle cutters or lids
- Paintbrush

* NOTE: To make flesh-coloured sugarpaste, use either "paprika" food colour paste or a mixture of yellow and pink sugarpastes.

Decorating Variation

He may look totally different to the doll but, essentially, this cheeky soccer player is constructed in exactly the same way. Dress him in your favourite team's colours. Follow the instructions up to step 6 (except you'll probably need to make the shirt a different colour — you don't see many soccer players in pink!) (Also, leave out the eyelashes.) Instead of a skirt, use four short stubby sausages of white sugarpaste for the shorts and the socks and two flesh-coloured sausage shapes for the legs. Add a football and a couple of discs of flesh-coloured sugarpaste for his ears.

6 To make the collar, thinly roll out 60 g (2 oz) white sugarpaste and cut out a strip about 3 x 15 cm (1 x 6 in). Make a partial cut through the centre and lay the collar around the doll's neck. The cut should automatically part at the front of the doll to form a collar (3).

7 To make the buttons, roll and squash three 5 g (⅛ oz) balls of white sugarpaste into three flattish discs. Stick them down the centre of the doll and press a couple of hollows into each button with the end of a paintbrush. Make two 100 g (3 ½ oz) ovals for her feet and stick onto the board (4).

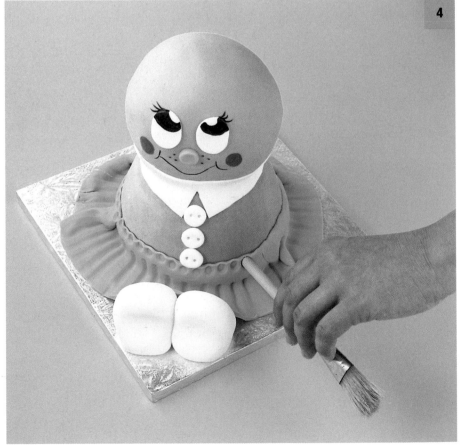

8 For the skirt, roll out 250 g (9 oz) pale blue sugarpaste. Cut out a large horseshoe shape. Press a paintbrush along the length of the skirt then wrap and stick the skirt around the base of the doll. The join should be at the back. Don't worry if it doesn't meet at the back as it won't be seen. Using the end of a paintbrush, poke a line of small hollows around the waistband to neaten it (4).

9 Make two 60 g (2 oz) flesh-coloured sugarpaste sausage shapes for the arms and stick into position on the body.

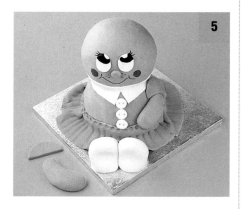

Roll 30 g (1 oz) pink sugarpaste into a ball for the sleeves. Flatten into a disc and cut in half. Stick one half over the top of each arm (5).

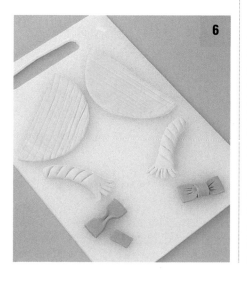

10 To make the hair, first roll out 120 g (4 oz) yellow sugarpaste and cut out a 15 cm (6 in) disc. Press lines across the circle using the back of a knife and cut in half (6). Stick in position on the front of the head. To make the plaits, divide 45 g (1½ oz) yellow sugarpaste in half and roll each half into a sausage. Flatten one end of each and cut a fringe. Press diagonal lines down both plaits and stick onto the head.

11 For the bows, cut two rectangles out of 15 g (½ oz) blue sugar-paste. Squeeze the centre of each rectangle and stick a small rectangle across it. Press a few lines either side of the centre and stick onto the plait.

12 To finish, roll out 250 g (8 oz) white sugarpaste and cut out a disc about 23 cm (9 in) in diameter for the mobcap. You can either do this free-hand or use a plate or cake board as a template. Frill around three-quarters of the outside of the disc by rolling a paintbrush backwards and forwards. Moisten the top of the doll's head and stick into position.

Candles

There should be enough room at the sides of the board to stick some candles inserted into thick sugarpaste discs (see page 27 for instructions).

Piggy bank

Here's a cake to appeal to anyone with an interest in money, from the youngest saver to the most hard-bitten of accountants. To make the pig more dramatic, paint a pattern on his back using food colours or stick on sugarpaste shapes.

1 Cover the cake board with green sugarpaste as explained on page 21 Trim and neaten the edges, then place the covered board to one side.

2 Slice and fill the centre of the cake with buttercream. Reassemble the cake and spread a layer of buttercream over the top and sides. Roll out and cover the cake with 250 g (8¾ oz) pink sugarpaste. Trim and neaten the base, then place the cake toward the rear of the covered cake board.

3 Make a simple floral pattern on the pig's back by pressing something circular (such as an piping nozzle or small circle cutter) into the sugarpaste while it is still pliable, then surrounding it with smaller circles made from a drinking straw *(fig 1)*.

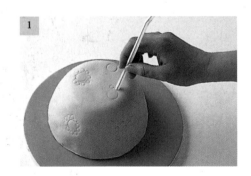

4 To make his face *(fig 2)*, thinly roll out 10 g (¼ oz) white sugarpaste. Cut out two disks about 2.5 cm (1 in) in diameter. Stick these to the front of the pig. Roll out the black sugarpaste and cut out two smaller disks and a small rectangle for the money slot. Stick the circles onto his eyes and the slot in the middle of his back. Finish off each eye with a tiny flattened ball of white sugarpaste as a highlight.

5 For his snout, roll and shape 40 g (1¾ oz) pink sugarpaste into a thick disk about 6.5 cm (2½ in) in diameter. Stick this to the front of his face. Don't use too much water

to do this or the snout will start to slide. Using the end of a wooden spoon, press two nostrils into the snout. Make a mouth either by pressing something circular into the sugarpaste (such as a cutter) or by using the back of a knife to make a curved line. Make two small cuts at each end of the mouth.

6 Make a tail by rolling about ⅛ oz pink fondant into a tapering sausage shape. Bend it into a curly tail shape and stick to the back of the pig.

7 To make the pig's ears, roll out 40 g (1¾ oz) pink ready-to-roll fondant to a thickness of about ¼ in. Cut out an ear shape, using the template if necessary. Scrunch up the leftover fondant and cut out a second ear. Stick the ears to the sides of the head, allowing them to fold over slightly at the top *(fig 3)*.

8 Cut one of the chocolate coins in half and press it into the money slot. A drop of water should be enough to hold it in place but you could use a dab of royal icing if you prefer. Arrange the rest of the coins around the board.

INGREDIENTS

- Icing (confectioners') sugar for rolling out
- 200g (7 oz) green sugarpaste (rolled fondant)
- Cake baked in a pudding bowl (see page 15)
- ½ quantity buttercream (see page 19)
- 340 g (12 oz) pink sugarpaste (rolled fondant)
- 10 g (¼ oz) white sugarpaste (rolled fondant)
- 20 g (¾ oz) black sugarpaste (rolled fondant)
- About 200 g (7 oz), or 4 small bags, of chocolate coins
- 15 ml (1 tbsp) royal icing (optional)

UTENSILS

- 25 cm (10 in) round cake board
- Water and paintbrush
- Rolling pin
- Small sharp knife
- Piping nozzle
- Drinking straw
- Wooden spoon
- Large circle cutter (optional)

TIP
If you don't have any royal icing readily available for sticking on the coins, use leftover buttercream instead – it will hold them in place just as well.

Christening cake

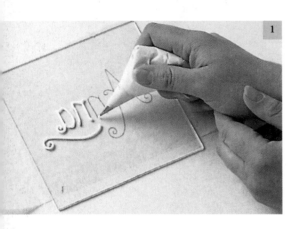

If you're worried about piping directly onto the top of this cake, two methods of writing in icing are also shown. Read the instructions in step 1 first and see which one suits you best.

1 If you feel confident enough to pipe the baby's name directly onto the top of the cake without following a guide, go straight to step 2. If you're not, then one of these two solutions might help.

(a) Do this after you have covered the cake with sugarpaste. Write the baby's name on a piece of greaseproof paper. Place the paper, right side up, on the top of the cake and using either a cocktail stick, dressmaking pin or scriber (this is a sugarcraft tool especially designed for the job), trace over the lettering. Lift off the greasproof paper and a scratched impression of the name should be left behind on the sugarpaste.

Place about 15 ml (1 tbsp) royal icing into a piping bag fitted with a number 2 piping nozzle and secure the end. Pipe over the lettering.

This method works best on a cake covered in sugarpaste that has been allowed to harden overnight. Otherwise it is very easy to dent the cake accidentally when leaning on it.

(b) Prepare this before you cover the cake with the sugarpaste.

Write the baby's name on greaseproof paper. Turn the paper over so that the writing is still visible but now reads back to front. Place a small piece of perspex over the greaseproof paper. Pipe over the name with royal icing onto the perspex *(fig 1)*.

Put to one side, leave to dry and go on to step 2.

2 Level the top of the cake. Turn it upside down and place on the cake board. Slice and fill the centre with buttercream. Reassemble the cake and buttercream the sides and top.

Dust the work surface with a little icing sugar and knead and roll out 500 g (1 lb 2 oz) yellow sugarpaste. Place this over the cake and carefully smooth it into position. Run over the surface with a cake smoother, if you have one, to iron out any bumps. Alternatively, use the flat of your hand. Trim away any excess sugarpaste from the base.

Lightly moisten the exposed cake board with a little water. Roll out 200 g (7 oz) yellow sugarpaste and cut out a strip approximately 61 cm (24 in) long and 3 cm (1¼ in) wide. Carefully roll up the sugarpaste strip, then unwind it to cover the cake board (see page 22). If you find this too time-consuming, you can leave the base uncovered.

■ INGREDIENTS

- Royal icing (see page 20)
- 20 cm (10 in) round sponge cake
- 1 quantity buttercream (see page 19)
- Icing (confectioners') sugar for rolling out
- 700 g (1 lb 9 oz) yellow sugarpaste (rolled fondant)
- 100 g (3½ oz) flesh-coloured sugarpaste (rolled fondant)
- 50 g (2 oz) light brown sugarpaste (rolled fondant)
- 50 g (2 oz) dark brown sugarpaste (rolled fondant)
- 35 g (1¼ oz) pale blue sugarpaste (rolled fondant)
- 15 g (½ oz) white sugarpaste (rolled fondant)
- Black food colouring
- 20 small candies

■ UTENSILS

- Greaseproof (waxed) paper
- Pencil
- Eraser
- Sheet of clear perspex (plexiglass) (about 20 cm x 13 cm / 8 in x 5 in) (optional)
- Pin or scriber (optional)
- Piping bags (see page 26 for details)
- Scissors
- Number 2 or 3 piping nozzles
- Clean damp cloth
- Carving knife
- 25 cm (10 in) round cake board
- Rolling pin
- Cake smoother (optional)
- Small sharp knife
- Water
- Medium and fine paintbrushes
- Cocktail stick (toothpick)
- 150 cm (60 in) white ribbon

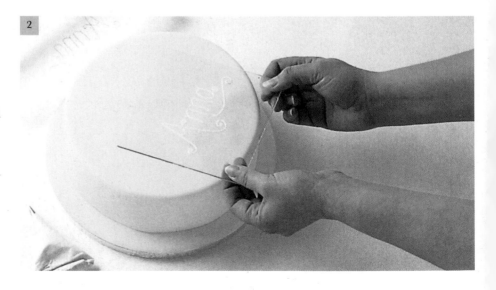

3

board. Starting from the back of the cake, hold the piping bag at a slight angle. Squeeze out a little royal icing, then release the pressure and pull slightly. Keep the tip of the nozzle in the icing all the time. Squeeze out a little more icing, release the pressure and pull (*fig 3*). Repeat all the way around the base of the cake.

You may wish to practice this technique on your work surface first if you are not too confident of your piping skills. Alternatively, pipe a simple line of dots or stick sweets on the cake instead.

5 All the babies, dressed or undressed, are composed of the same six basic shapes (*fig 4*). To make the baby's body, roll 20 g (¾ oz) flesh-coloured sugarpaste into a conical shape. Make the head by rolling 5 g (⅛ oz) of flesh-coloured sugarpaste into a small ball. Stick in place with a little water (*fig 5*).

Make the baby's legs by rolling approximately 10 g (¼ oz) flesh-coloured sugarpaste into a sausage. Cut this in two,

3 If using the second method of writing, gently touch the royal icing on the perspex to check that it has dried. If it still feels soft, then place a bit of cling film over the top of the cake to stop the sugarpaste surface from hardening too much before the piping is ready. (The sugarpaste has to be soft enough to take an impression.) When the piping feels hard to the touch, turn the perspex over and press the lettering into the top of the cake (*fig 2*). Carefully pull it away. The baby's name should now be visible as an impression. Pipe over the name with white royal icing, using a number 2 nozzle.

4 When the name is on the top of the cake, pipe a "snail trail" around the base of the cake to hide the join between cake and

5

4

TIP

To avoid damaging the rolled fondant cake, you may find it easier to make the models of the babies away from the cake and then stick them in position once they are finished.

then gently bend the end of each one to form a foot. Stick these in whatever position you wish.

For the arms, take about 5 g (⅛ oz) sugarpaste and roll into a sausage. Cut in two and flatten one end of each half to make a hand. Stick these against the body. Thinly roll out a little white sugarpaste and cut out a tiny triangle. Stick this on as a nappy (diaper).

Paint the facial details with black food colouring and a fine paintbrush, and stick two tiny dots of sugarpaste either side of the head for the ears and one in the middle of the face for a nose. To make a frilly mop hat, simply cut out a thin disk of white sugarpaste and roll a cocktail stick around the edge to frill it *(fig 6)*. Stick onto the back of the head and roll a tiny bit of yellow sugarpaste into a curl and stick onto the forehead.

6 Make as many or as few babies as you want (or you have time for), altering the positions of the hands and feet and giving each one an individual expression and different hair colour.

Use the same shapes for the baby in the romper suit, but use coloured sugarpaste for the arms, legs and body to look like the clothing.

7 To complete the cake, stick small sweets around the top and the board, and tie a bow around the sides as the perfect finishing touch.

Decorating variation

As you can see, this cake works just as well in a different colour. If you prefer something paler, leave the base of the cake white and colour the piping instead. If you find it difficult to tie a bow, leave it off and add a couple more babies and sweets to fill the space instead.

Caterpillar

This is such an easy cake to put together. If you haven't time to bake fairy cakes, cheat and use packs of shop-bought cakes instead. If it's the thought of all that piped buttercream that worries you, then sandwich the cakes together with "splodges" instead!

1 Lay all your cakes roughly in position on the board to check whether there are enough and also to work out the colours. Note that the "head" cake stands on top of another cake to give it added height.

2 If using a piping nozzle , cut a small triangle off the pointed end of the piping bag (see page 24) and insert the nozzle. Place a couple of tablespoons of buttercream into the bag and fold the end over twice to close it. If you're not using a nozzle, place the buttercream into the bag, close it and then snip a triangle off the end. Starting from the centre of the fairy cakes, pipe a spiral on top of each cake (1). If you find this too tricky, just spoon a dollop of buttercream on the top of the cake instead!

3 Stick the cakes in position around the board as soon as you've buttercreamed them (2). If you leave them too long, the buttercream will start to dry out and lose its sticking ability.

4 To make the caterpillar's face, begin with the eyes. Use about 5 g (⅛ oz) white sugarpaste. Pull off a tiny bit and put to one side. Divide the rest in half and roll into two balls. Squash the two balls to form two flat discs and press on to the caterpillar's head.

Keep a small piece of the black sugarpaste to one side, then make two smaller black sugarpaste discs in the same way for the pupils and roll the reserved white sugarpaste into two dots for the highlights.

5 From the rest of the black sugarpaste, make a small button for his nose and a short sausage shape for his mouth. Stick into position on the face.

6 To make each foot, roll about 15 g (½ oz) white sugarpaste into an oval. It will get a little busy in the middle of the cake if you allow two feet per cake so limit it to just five or six in the centre. Stick each foot as required onto the board with a little water.

7 Cut a short length (about 8 cm/3 in) of liquorice bootlace for each foot. Using the end of a paintbrush, poke a hole in a foot and a hole in the top of the corresponding cake, then insert the liquorice leg (3). Work around the cake.

8 Finally insert two lollipops into the caterpillar's head for his feelers and spoon the green-coloured dessicated coconut around the board.

Carol suggests

If you can't get hold of liquorice bootlaces or anything similar you could substitute chocolate sticks or sections of raw, dried spaghetti instead. Alternatively use lollipops, upside down without the sugarpaste feet.

INGREDIENTS

- About 14 coloured fairy cakes (see page 15)
- 1 quantity buttercream (see page 19)
- 350 g (12 oz) white sugarpaste (rolled fondant)
- 15 g (½ oz) black sugarpaste (rolled fondant)
- 3 thin liquorice bootlaces or similar (colour of your choice)
- 2 lollipops
- 45 g (1½ oz) green-coloured desiccated (shredded) coconut (see page 18)

UTENSILS

- 30 cm (12 in) round cake board
- Piping (decorating) bag (optional)
- Star piping nozzle (optional)
- Scissors
- Paintbrush

Sports car

This will suit anyone with a passion for fast cars and will disappear off the tea table speedily too! It's also very versatile — see how the basic shape can be adapted into an aeroplane (page 107). The rocks double up as candle holders.

1 Stand the cake up with the thinnest part at the bottom. Cut two triangular pieces away from the sides to form the bonnet. Cut a slope into the top of the bonnet too. Level the remaining top section of the cake where the driver will eventually sit and round all the top edges slightly to form the basic shape (*fig 1*).

Slice and fill the middle of the cake with buttercream. Reassemble and place it diagonally on the cake board. Spread a thin layer of buttercream over the top and sides of the cake.

2 Dust the worksurface with icing sugar and knead and roll out the green sugarpaste. Carefully lift this over the cake and gently smooth into position. Trim and neaten the base.

3 To make the driver, first roll 100 g (3½ oz) of flesh-coloured sugarpaste into a flattish oval shape (*fig 2*). Stick this with a little water towards the back of the car.

Roll 70 g (2½ oz) of brown sugarpaste into a ball then flatten the base to make a semi-circular shape for the driver's helmet. Stick this on top of his head. Roll out about another 10 g (¼ oz) of brown sugarpaste and cut out a thin, flat semi-circle. Stick this to the front of the helmet to form the brim (*fig 3*).

INGREDIENTS

- Cake baked in loaf tin (see page 15 for details)
- 1 quantity buttercream (see page 19)
- Icing (confectioners') sugar for rolling out
- 250 g (9 oz) green sugarpaste (rolled fondant)
- 130 g (4½ oz) flesh-coloured sugarpaste (rolled fondant)
- 110 g (3¾ oz) brown sugarpaste (rolled fondant)
- 120 g (4 oz) white sugarpaste (rolled fondant)
- 150 g (5 oz) black sugarpaste (rolled fondant)
- 40 g (1½ oz) grey sugarpaste (rolled fondant)
- 40 g (1½ oz) cream sugarpaste (rolled fondant)
- Black and green food colour pastes
- 60 g (2 oz) desiccated (shredded) coconut

UTENSILS

- Carving knife
- Palette knife (metal spatula)
- 25 cm (10 in) square cake board
- Rolling pin
- Small sharp knife
- Water and paintbrush
- Circle cutters or similar
- 2 small bowls

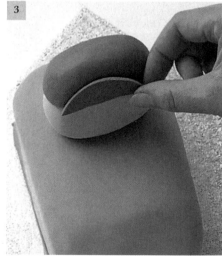

4 For the eyes, roll out 10 g (¼ oz) of white sugarpaste to a thickness of 5 mm (¼ in) and cut out two discs about 2 cm (¾ in) in diameter. If you don't have a circle cutter this size and can't find a lid or anything else to use as a cutter, simply divide the icing into two, roll each half into a ball, then squash each ball down to the right size. Finish off the eyes by sticking two tiny flattened balls of black sugarpaste onto the

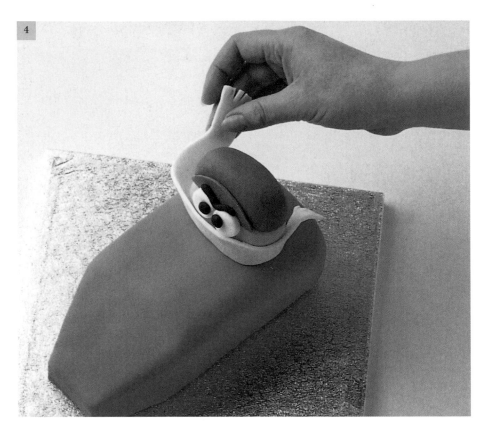

white for his pupils and a small sausage of black over the top for his eyebrows.

5 To make the scarf, roll out the cream sugarpaste. Cut into a strip about 28 cm x 2.5 cm (11 in x 1 in). Cut a fringe into both ends and paint a line of water around the driver's neck. Lay the scarf into position (*fig 4*). Tweak the ends up slightly into a jaunty, 'blowing in the wind' angle.

6 Roll a pea-sized ball of flesh-coloured sugarpaste and stick onto the driver's face

for his nose. Knead and shape about 10 g (¼ oz) of grey sugarpaste into a thickish semi-circle for the steering wheel. Stick this in front of the driver.

Roll 20 g (¾ oz) of black sugarpaste into a sausage about 25 cm (10 in) long. Starting from the back, lay and stick this on top of the car, around the driver (*fig 5*).

7 To make the driver's arms, roll about 15 g (½ oz) of brown sugarpaste into a sausage about 10 cm (4 in) long. Cut it in half. Make two partial cuts in the centre of each

arm at the elbow and bend each one into a right-angle. Stick an arm on each side of the body.

Finish off the arms by sticking on a pair of hands made from small flattened circles of flesh-coloured sugarpaste. Arrange the hands so that they hold onto the steering wheel.

8 To make the ear flaps for the helmet, roll out approximately 15 g (½ oz) of brown sugarpaste. Cut out two small oval shapes. If you find cutting out an oval using the tip of your knife too fiddly, cut out a circle instead using a small lid or circle cutter, then gently pull it into shape. Another method is to cut out a rectangle, slice off the corners and gently smooth the edges into an oval.

When you have made your oval shapes, stick one either side of the helmet for the flaps (*fig 6*). Next, cut two tiny strips for his helmet straps and stick one on either flap.

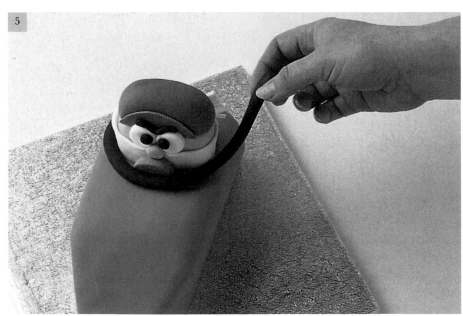

TIP

To personalize your car, write the recipient's name, age or a short message on the number plate using black food colour and a paintbrush.

9 To make the wheels, roll out about 125 g (4¼ oz) of black sugarpaste to a thickness of about 5 mm (¼ in). Cut out two discs about 6 cm (2¼ in) in diameter. Scrunch up the leftover icing. Re-roll it and cut out another two discs. Stick the wheels into position (fig 7).

Roll out about 10 g (¼ oz) of white sugarpaste and cut out four smaller and much thinner discs. If you haven't got anything suitable to cut out a circle with, simply divide the sugarpaste into four. Roll each quarter into a ball and flatten to the required size. These circles form the centres of the wheels. Stick them neatly into position.

10 For the bumpers, roll 30 g (1 oz) of grey sugarpaste out to a thickness of about 5 mm (¼ in). Cut out two strips. The first should measure about 8 cm (3 in) long by 2 cm (¾ in) wide. Stick this around the front of the car. The back bumper should measure about 15 cm x 2 cm (6 in x ¾ in). Stick this into place too.

11 To make the headlights, take another 10 g (¼ oz) of grey sugarpaste and roll this into an egg shape. Cut it in half and stick both halves to the front of the bonnet. Thinly roll out about 20 g (¾ oz) of white sugarpaste and cut out two small discs. Stick one disc onto the front of each headlight.

Also cut out two small rectangles for the number plates and stick them to the front and back of the car.

12 Place 20 g (¾ oz) of the desiccated coconut in one of the bowls and colour it green by mixing in a little green food colour paste. Colour the rest grey in another bowl with a little black food paste.

Decorating variation

To adapt the car into an aeroplane, the same basic body shape was covered with grey sugarpaste. The wings and tail were made out of grey-coloured gelatin icing (see page 20) and allowed to harden overnight. (Turn the components over after about 4-5 hours to allow the undersides to dry out as well.) They were attached to the body of the plane with royal icing and supported by balls of scrunched up clingfilm placed underneath the wings while drying in position. Add a propeller to the front of the plane. Decorate the nose of the plane and the wings with circles of coloured sugarpaste. The cake board was covered in pale blue sugarpaste and decorated with white cut-out clouds and birds painted in black food colour.

Lightly moisten the exposed cake board with a few drops of water. Carefully spoon the grey coconut immediately around the car then spoon the green over the edges. To make things easier and quicker, you could colour all the coconut just one shade if you prefer.

13 Finally, to make the rocks, partially knead about 80 g (2¾ oz) of white sugarpaste and about 20 g (¾ oz) of black together for a marbled effect. Pull off irregular sized lumps and stick these along the side of the road. These rocks can also be used as candle holders.

Chocolate box

A wonderful cake suitable for all sorts of occasions
– birthdays, Valentine's day, Mother's day, anniversaries
or any chocoholic type of day (and you don't need much of an excuse
for those!).

■ INGREDIENTS

- 15 cm (6 in) round sponge cake
- ½ quantity buttercream (see page 19)
- Icing (confectioners') sugar for rolling out
- 100 g (3 oz) black sugarpaste (rolled fondant)
- 300 g (10 oz) pink sugarpaste (rolled fondant)
- 30 g (1 oz) bag white chocolate buttons
- 227 g (½ lb) box milk chocolates
- 200 g (7 oz) white sugarpaste (rolled fondant)

■ UTENSILS

- Carving knife
- 23 cm (9 in) round cake board
- Rolling pin
- 15 cm (6 in) round thin cake board
- Small sharp knife
- Ruler
- Heart-shaped cutter
- Drinking straw
- Water and paintbrush
- 70 cm (30 in) ribbon

1   Level the cake if necessary then turn it upside down and place onto the cake board. Slice and fill the centre with buttercream and spread a thin layer of buttercream around the top and sides.

2   Knead and roll out all the black sugarpaste on a work surface dusted with icing sugar. Using the thin 15 cm (6 in) cake board as a template, cut out a black disc and lay this on top of the cake. Clean your hands, rolling pin and worksurface to avoid getting black sooty smudges everywhere.

3   Measure the height of the cake. Sprinkle the worksurface with icing sugar and roll out 200 g (7 oz) of pink sugarpaste so that you can cut out a strip about 46 cm (18 in) long and about 1 cm (½ in) wider than the depth of your cake (this cake measured about 9 cm/3½ in). Roll the icing up like a bandage, making sure it is not too tight or you will have problems unwinding it. Dust with more icing sugar if it seems to be sticking and then unwind it around the side of the cake (fig 1).

   If the icing won't stick, it probably means the previous buttercream covering around the sides has dried out so simply spread another thin layer to provide better adhesion. Neaten and trim away any excess from the base and the join.

4   Using a heart-shaped cutter and a drinking straw, press a pattern around the side of the box.

5   Carefully paint a light line of water around the inside edge of the black disc. Neatly press a line of white chocolate buttons vertically into the black icing, allowing them to rest against the pink sugarpaste (fig 2).

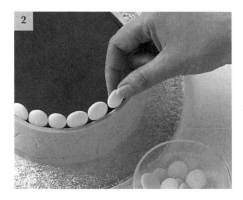

6   Arrange the chocolates in the top of the box, securing them in position with dabs of buttercream. Unfortunately, this arrangement uses up most of a 227 g (½ lb) box of milk chocolates, leaving only a couple left over for the cook. Stick one of these on top of the chocolates to support the lid and sample the leftovers – all for purely professional taste testing purposes, of course!

7   Moisten the top and sides of the thin cake board with a little water, roll out and cover with 100 g (3 oz) of pink sugarpaste. Trim and neaten the edges and press the heart cutter and drinking straw into the icing to echo the pattern around the sides. Place the lid to one side temporarily whilst you cover the base to avoid it from getting damaged.

8   Moisten the exposed cake board with a little water. Knead and roll 200 g (7 oz) of white sugarpaste into a strip. Roll it up, then unwind it around the board allowing it to fall into folds like fabric as you go. Press the icing down neatly at the edges of the board and trim away any excess.

9   Place a small dab of buttercream on top of the highest chocolate. Place the lid in position on top.

10 Make a bow out of the ribbon and attach this to the cake with a little more buttercream.

TIP

For a completely edible box (if you have time), you could make the lid out of pink-coloured gelatin icing as shown on page 20 and decorate this with an icing bow.

Birthday Picnic

Here's a birthday picnic that looks good enough to eat! For an added personal touch, try to make the child look as much like the recipient as possible.

The little elephant model would also work equally as well on a leaving cake with the caption "We'll never forget you!"

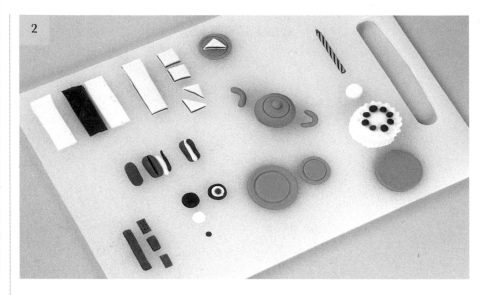

1 Begin by covering the board with the green sugarpaste, using the "all-in-one" method shown on page 21 and place to one side. Level the top of the cake and turn it upside-down so that you have a nice, flat surface on the top. Slice horizontally and fill the centre with buttercream. Spread a liberal layer of buttercream around the sides of the cake and a thin layer over the top. Using a fish slice, to stop your fingers getting sticky, lift and place the cake in the centre of the covered board.

2 To make the tablecloth, first measure the height of your cake and double the number. Add this figure to the diameter across the top of the cake (in my case, this came to 35 cm/14 in). You will now need either a round plate or cake board with a diameter the same as this new

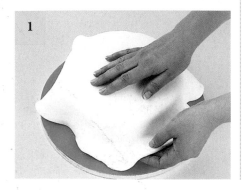

measurement (if you have neither, cut out a card template instead). Roll out 600 g (1 lb 5 oz) white sugarpaste. Place your template on top and cut round it using the tip of a sharp knife. Carefully lift up the sugarpaste disc, (wiggle a long palette knife under it to loosen it if it sticks) and place on top of the cake. Allow the sides to fall into neat pleats and folds, tweaking them where necessary (1). Place the cake to one side.

3 For the crockery, use a set of circle cutters, icing nozzles or small lids as cutters. Roll out 30 g (1 oz) pale blue sugarpaste and cut out one disc 5 cm (2 in) wide, four disks with a 4 cm (1½ in) diameter and four disks 2.5 cm (1 in) wide. Re-roll the icing as necessary. The plates can be left plain or you could paint on a coloured pattern and press a slightly smaller cutter or lid just inside each disc to leave a circular imprint (2).

INGREDIENTS

- 20 cm (8 in) round cake
- 1 quantity buttercream (see page 19)
- Icing (confectioners') sugar for rolling out
- 300 g (10 oz) green sugarpaste (rolled fondant)
- 700 g (1lb 9 oz) white sugarpaste (rolled fondant)
- 100 g (3½ oz) pale blue sugarpaste (rolled fondant)
- 15 g (½ oz) red sugarpaste (rolled fondant)
- 90 g (3 oz) dark brown sugarpaste (rolled fondant)
- 15 g (½ oz) light brown sugarpaste (rolled fondant)
- 120 g (4 oz) grey sugarpaste (rolled fondant)
- 4 strands raw, dried spaghetti
- 30 g (1 oz) black sugarpaste (rolled fondant)
- 60 g (2 oz) dark pink sugarpaste (rolled fondant)
- 30 g (1 oz) yellow sugarpaste (rolled fondant)
- 30 g (1 oz) flesh-coloured sugarpaste (rolled fondant)
- 75 g (2½ oz) pale pink sugarpaste (rolled fondant)
- Red food colour paste

UTENSILS

- 30 cm (12 in) round cake board
- Rolling pin
- Fish slice (pancake turner) (optional)
- Ruler or tape measure
- 35 cm (14 in) cake board or plate (see step 2)
- Small, sharp knife
- Palette knife (metal spatula)
- Assorted circle cutters or lids
- Birthday cake candle
- Large drinking straw
- Cocktail stick
- Paintbrush
- Piping nozzle (any size)
- Five petal flower cutter (optional)

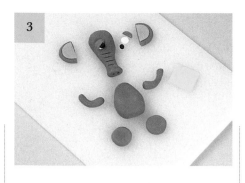

4 To make the birthday cake, roll 30 g (1 oz) white sugarpaste into a thick disc. Using the end of a paintbrush, poke and drag a series of dents around the base of the disc. Turn the disc upside-down and repeat.

Stick the cake onto the largest plate and eight tiny red sugarpaste balls around the top, for glacé cherries (2). Stick a small ball of white sugarpaste in the centre and stick a candle on the top. Place to one side.

5 For the sandwiches, take 10 g (¼ oz) white sugarpaste and 5 g (⅛ oz) red sugarpaste. Divide the white sugarpaste in half and roll all three pieces of sugarpaste into thin strips and stick on top of each other with the red in the centre. Cut into a rectangle then into squares. Divide each square into quarters diagonally (2).

Arrange and stick about five sandwiches onto one of the larger plates with water. Place another couple of sandwiches on two of the smaller plates. Take a "bite" out of one sandwich using the end of a drinking straw and place this, the plate and any leftover sandwiches to one side.

6 To make the iced buns, roll 5 g (⅛ oz) dark brown sugarpaste into eight ball shapes, then flatten each one to make a disc. Top each bun with a smaller flattened disc of white sugarpaste and a minute ball of red sugarpaste to look like a cherry.

Stick seven buns onto a serving plate and one onto a small plate. Place to one side.

7 For the shortbread, roll out 10 g (¼ oz) light brown sugarpaste and cut into a rectangle. Divide into about ten smaller rectangles and, using the point n a cocktail stick, poke six tiny holes into the top of each biscuit. Pile the shortbread biscuits up on a serving plate and place to one side.

8 To make the iced donuts, divide 10 g (¼ oz) light brown sugarpaste into eight pieces. Roll each piece into an oval and partially slice through each oval lengthways. Fill the centre of each donut by lying a very thin string of red and white sugarpaste down the length of the bun. Again, place to the side to decorate the cake with later.

9 To make a teapot, use 30 g (1 oz) pale blue sugarpaste. Pull off a little for the handle and spout and roll the rest into a ball. Using a piping nozzle or something similar, press a little circle into the top of the ball. Roll a little of the leftover icing into a tiny ball and stick on top of the teapot. Divide the rest in two and roll into two thin sausage shapes. Stick one on the front of the pot, bending the tip forward to look like a spout. Bend the other into a semi-circle for its handle and stick on the back and place to one side.

10 For the elephant's body, roll 60 g (2 oz) grey sugarpaste into a cone and insert a couple of short lengths of spaghetti in the top. Make two thick grey 5 g (⅛ oz) discs for his feet and stick these onto his tummy (3). Using a large (or jumbo – very apt) drinking straw, press four semi-circles into the top of each foot to look like his toes. Roll 30 g (1 oz) grey sugarpaste into a tapering sausage shape for his head and flatten the thicker end slightly. It should now look a bit like a tennis racquet. Stick the head onto the body. Press a few lines into the trunk with the back of a knife and a couple of nostrils with the end of a paintbrush.

11 To make his eyes, stick two white and two smaller black sugarpaste discs onto his face. Make another disk from grey sugarpaste and cut it in half. Stick one half over each eye. For his ears, roll 10 g (¼ oz) grey sugarpaste into a ball then flatten slightly. Repeat using a smaller dark pink sugarpaste ball. Place the pink shape on top of the grey and squash the two together. Cut the disc in half and stick one ear on either side of his head. Make a tiny yellow sugarpaste square for his napkin. Roll 5 g (⅛ oz) grey sugarpaste into two sausage shapes for his arms. Fold the napkin over the end of one of the arms and stick onto the body. Stick the other arm in place. Place to one side.

12 To make the boy figure (see page 23 for a girl figure), roll 30 g (1 oz) white sugarpaste into a cone for his body (4). For his legs, roll 30 g (1 oz) blue sugarpaste into a sausage, cut in half and stick in place. Stick a yellow sugarpaste serviette onto his front and insert a short length of dried spaghetti into his body. Roll 15 g (½ oz) flesh-coloured sugarpaste into a ball for his head and stick onto the body. Poke a round mouth and add two tiny white and black sugarpaste discs for his eyes and a small flesh-coloured nose.

13 The boy's hair is made by rolling and cutting out a small dark brown sugarpaste rectangle. Press lines down its length with the back of a knife and lay the strip over the top of the boy's head. Cut out tiny rectangles and make small cuts along one of its longer sides to make a fringe. Roll a little flesh-coloured sugarpaste into two tiny balls for his ears and stick onto the side of his head. Poke a little hollow into both with the end of a paintbrush.

14 Divide and roll about 10 g (¼ oz) white sugarpaste into two small sausage shapes for his arms. Bend both at the elbow and stick onto the body. Stick the sandwich, with a bite taken out of it, onto his chest between the arms and, using two tiny flattened discs of flesh-coloured sugarpaste as hands, position these as though holding the sandwich. Finally, make two 5 g (⅛ oz) black sugarpaste ovals for feet.

15 Place the boy, elephant, cake, teapot and plates (except for one small one) on top of the cake. "Glue" them in place with a little water. To make the teddy, roll 30 g (1 oz) pale pink sugarpaste into a cone (5). Stick on the front edge of the cake. Insert a length of spaghetti into the body. Divide 15 g (½ oz) pink sugarpaste in half and roll into two sausage shapes for his legs. Bend the ends up to form feet and stick

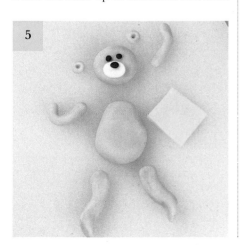

onto the body so that they dangle over the edge of the cake. Make a yellow sugarpaste serviette and a 15 g (½ oz) pink sugarpaste ball for his head and stick both into place. Add a small white icing oval for his muzzle and tiny black sugarpaste eyes and nose. Stick these slightly off-centre as though he's looking downwards. Stick two pink sugarpaste balls on his head for his ears and make a hole in each with the end of a paintbrush. Make two small pink sugarpaste sausages for his arms and stick into place.

16 To make the chimp, roll 30 g (1 oz) dark brown sugarpaste into a cone and stick on the board, using the cake for support. Pull one third off a 15 g (½ oz) lump of dark brown sugarpaste and form an oval for his back foot (6). Stick into position bending the top of the foot forwards slightly. Mould

the remaining icing into a tennis racquet shape. Bend the end up to make a foot and stick onto the side of the monkey. Roll about 15 g (½ oz) dark brown icing into a ball for his head and stick in place.

17 Flatten a small banana-shaped piece of flesh-coloured icing and stick onto the face for his muzzle. Press something curved such as the edge of a lid or cutter into the muzzle to make a mouth. Add white discs and black icing dots for eyes and a tiny flesh-coloured dot for a nose. Finally, roll about 5 g (⅛ oz) brown sugarpaste into two long, thin sausages for his arms. Stick one as though reaching up to the table and the other around one of the spare sandwiches. Stick the remaining plate of food on the ground by his side.

18 For the flowers to decorate the cake, roll out about 50 g (1¾ oz) pink sugarpaste and cut out about eight flowers using the petal cutter (see page 25 in Basic Techniques section for instructions). Finally, paint red food colour stripes onto the tablecloth (7).

Candles

If you only need a few candles, make the miniature cake larger and stand them in that. Alternatively place the candles into icing rocks around the board (see page 27). Keep well away from the sides of the cake.

Gardener's delight

A novel cake for budding gardeners. It could be decorated with flowers instead if you prefer — see page 27 for effective but extremely fast flowers. If you're not keen on marzipan, this cake looks just as effective made up in sugarpaste.

INGREDIENTS

- Flowerpot-shaped cake (see step 1)
- 1 quantity buttercream (see page 19)
- Icing (confectioners') sugar for rolling out
- 920 g (2 lb) white marzipan
- Paprika, red, green, dark brown, black, orange and yellow food colour pastes
- 60 g (2 oz) dark brown sugar

UTENSILS

- 23 cm (9 in) round cake board
- Carving knife
- Palette knife (metal spatula)
- Rolling pin
- Tape measure
- Water and paintbrush
- Small sharp knife

1 The easiest way to make a cake of this shape is to bake the cake itself in a new 15 cm (6 in) terracotta plant pot. Simply wash the pot out, grease and line it with greaseproof paper. Use the same amounts given on page 10 for a 15 cm (6 in) square cake. Level the top of the cake and turn upside down so the widest part sits on the board. Slice and fill the centre with buttercream and spread extra buttercream around the top and sides.

2 Colour 550 g (1 lb 4 oz) marzipan terracotta using paprika food colour paste. If you can't obtain paprika colour, use a mixture of red, yellow and a hint of brown. Roll out 400 g (14 oz) on a worksurface dusted with icing sugar and cover the cake. Smooth over the top and sides and trim any excess from the base.

3 Re-knead the excess into the rest of the terracotta-coloured marzipan. Roll it out and cut out a strip about 46 cm x 4 cm (18 in x 1½ in). Paint a line of water around the base of the cake. Wind up the marzipan strip like a bandage. Then, starting from the back, unwind it around the base of the cake so it resembles the lip of a real flowerpot (*fig 1*). Neaten the join.

4 To make the tomatoes, colour 50 g (1¾ oz) marzipan red. Roll into two balls and make a dent in the top of each one with the end of a paintbrush. Roll out about 5 g (⅛ oz) green-coloured marzipan and cut out two rough star shapes. Stick one on the top of each tomato with a little water (*fig 2*).

5 For the potatoes, roll 120 g (4 oz) of white marzipan into two misshapen oval shapes. Leave them like this for the moment as they are easier to paint once in position.

6 For the carrots, colour 60 g (2 oz) of marzipan orange. Divide into three and roll into carrot shapes. Press a few lines across the top using the back of a knife. Roll out 5 g (⅛ oz) of green marzipan and cut out three irregular rectangles. Make cuts down almost the whole length of each shape and fringe. Stick one on each carrot.

7 For the peas, simply colour about 10 g (¼ oz) of marzipan a pale green colour and roll into small balls.

8 For the pepper, colour 80 g (2¾ oz) of marzipan yellow and roll into a conical shape. Press small grooves into the sides and top and finish with some green marzipan bent into a stalk.

9 Arrange the vegetables around the base of the flowerpot, securing them with a little water. Make sure the join on the lip of the flowerpot is hidden at the back. Moisten the exposed cake board with a little water and spoon the dark brown sugar around the board to look like soil.

10 Paint the potatoes with a wash of watered-down brown food colour. Finish with tiny dots of black food colour and also paint a black circle on the top of the cake to look like the hole in the top of the flowerpot.

11 Roll out 40 g (1½ oz) of green marzipan and cut out some leaves. Press a few veins in each one using the back of a knife and stick these around the flowerpot.

Golfing star

A fun way of incorporating a person's favourite sport into a design is to base the cake itself on a piece of equipment such as a golf bag or a tennis racquet, then make a small model of the recipient dressed in the appropriate outfit.

1 Moisten the cake board with a little water. Sprinkle some icing sugar onto the worksurface and knead the green sugarpaste until it becomes pliable. Begin to roll it out into a thick, flattish disk, then lift and place the sugarpaste on the cake board. Continue to roll the icing up to and over the edges of the board. Trim and neaten the edges.

If you possess one, run a cake smoother over the surface of the board to iron out any lumps and bumps. Alternatively, use the flat of your hand and strategically position the cake, figure and golf clubs over the worst bits later! Place the covered board to one side.

2 Cut the cake into shape by slicing about 5 cm (2 in) off one side. Place this against one of the now shorter sides to increase the length of the bag. Now cut the cake into a more recognisable bag shape by making two diagonal cuts at the top of the bag to give it a tapering neck and also cut a slope into the neck of the bag (*fig 1*). Round all the corners slightly.

3 Slice and fill the middle of the cake with a layer of buttercream, then spread a thin covering of buttercream over the top and sides. Wipe away any crumbs from the worksurface and dust with icing sugar.

Knead and roll out 300 g (10½ oz) of white sugarpaste. Lift and place over the cake. Smooth the icing into position and trim away any excess from the base. Carefully lift the cake and place on the covered cake board. (You may find using a fish slice to lift the cake helps to prevent fingerprints on the icing.)

4 Roll and shape about 20 g (¾ oz) of grey sugarpaste into a sort of tennis racquet shape. Bend the large, rounded end over to one side to make a golf club and stick onto the board at the neck of the bag.

To make the wooden club, roll 40 g (1½ oz) of brown sugarpaste into a more rounded club shape. Stick a small flat oval of grey sugarpaste onto the top of the club and stick into position. Press a few lines into the top of the first club using the back of a knife (*fig 2*).

■ **INGREDIENTS**

- Icing (confectioners') sugar for rolling out
- 300 g (10½ oz) green sugarpaste (rolled fondant)
- 15 cm (6 in) square cake
- 1 quantity buttercream (see page 19)
- 360 g (12½ oz) white sugarpaste (rolled fondant)
- 50 g (2 oz) grey sugarpaste (rolled fondant)
- 70 g (2¼ oz) dark brown sugarpaste (rolled fondant)
- 90 g (3¼ oz) red sugarpaste (rolled fondant)
- 50 g (2 oz) light brown sugarpaste (rolled fondant)
- 40 g (1½ oz) yellow sugarpaste (rolled fondant)
- 80 g (2¾ oz) blue sugarpaste (rolled fondant)
- 30 g (1 oz) flesh-coloured sugarpaste (rolled fondant)
- 10 g (¼ oz) black sugarpaste (rolled fondant)

■ **UTENSILS**

- 30 cm (12 in) round cake board
- Water
- Paintbrush
- Rolling pin
- Small sharp knife
- Cake smoother (optional)
- Carving knife
- Fish slice (pancake turner) (optional)
- Palette knife (metal spatula)
- Piping nozzle

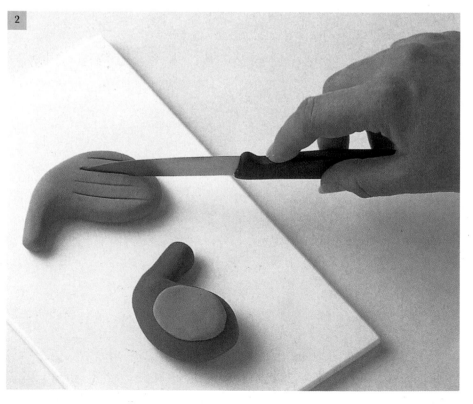

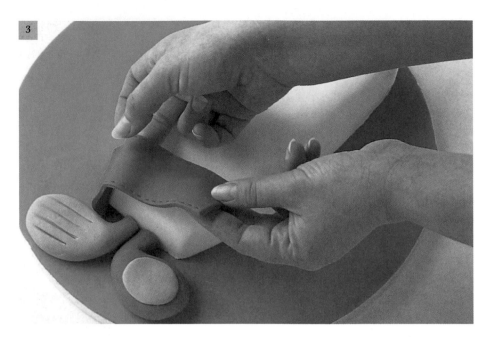

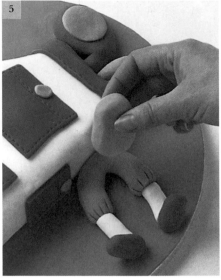

5 Roll out 20 g (¾ oz) of red sugarpaste and cut out a strip about 2.5 cm x 13 cm (1 in x 5 in). Make a series of small cuts along the two longer sides using just the tip of your knife to look like stitching. Lightly moisten the back of the strip with a little water and lay this over the base of the golf clubs and the neck of the bag (*fig 3*).

6 Roll out a further 70 g (2½ oz) of red sugarpaste and cut out four rectangles of varying sizes. Stick two on the front of the bag and two on the sides. Press the back of a knife across each one to leave a line looking like a flap. Using the tip of your knife again, 'stitch' around each pocket (*fig 4*). Finish off each pocket with a

button made from a small flattened ball of grey sugarpaste.

7 To make the golfer himself, begin with his legs. Roll about 40 g (1½ oz) of light brown sugarpaste into a sausage about 13 cm (5 in) long. Slightly bend the sausage into a 'U' shape and press a few lines into both ends to look like folds in the fabric. Stick this on the board towards the neck of the bag. Roll 20 g (¾ oz) of yellow sugarpaste into a sausage and cut in half. Stick one onto the end of each leg for his socks. Roll two 10 g (¼ oz) lumps of dark brown sugarpaste into two oval shapes for his feet and stick one on the end of each sock.

Make a body by rolling about 40 g (1¾ oz) of blue sugarpaste into a cone and stick this on top of the legs (*fig 5*).

8 To make the arms, roll 20 g (¾ oz) of blue sugarpaste into a sausage and cut in half. Stick one arm either side of the body, allowing them to rest on the legs and the side of the golf bag itself. Slightly flatten a small ball of blue sugarpaste to make a thickish disk for the golfer's polo neck (*fig 6*). Stick this on top of the body.

9 Make a head by rolling 10 g (¼ oz) of flesh-coloured sugarpaste into a ball. Stick this onto the neck. Give him a smiling mouth by pressing a piping nozzle or something similar into the lower part of the face and pulling it slightly downwards. His eyes are made by sticking two small disks of white sugarpaste onto his face.

Stick two smaller disks of blue onto the white and top with two even smaller discs of black sugarpaste. Stick a tiny ball

TIP
Personalize the figure by colouring the hair and eyes the same colour as the recipient's. Add any distinguishing features too, such as glasses, a beard or long hair.

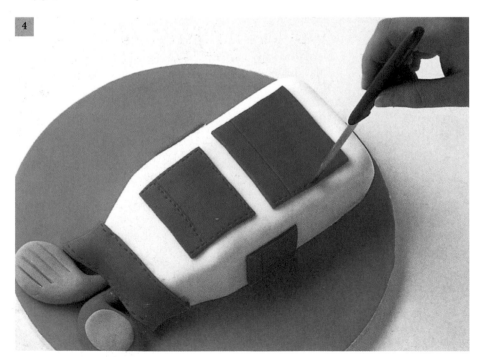

of flesh-coloured sugarpaste onto the face for his nose and two on either side of the head for his ears. Press the end of a paintbrush into each ear to leave a small hollow. Stick a small oval of flesh-coloured sugarpaste onto the end of each arm for his hands.

10 Make hair by sticking a couple of tiny bits of light brown sugarpaste to the top of the head. To make the cap, roll 10 g (¼ oz) of yellow sugarpaste into a flattish oval shape. Tweak the front into a peak and press lines across the top in a sort of star shape. Top with a tiny ball of yellow sugarpaste and stick on the top of the head. Decorate the front of the jumper and both socks with small, contrasting squares of blue and yellow sugarpaste.

11 To make the strap, thinly roll out 50 g (2 oz) white sugarpaste and cut out a strip about 30 cm x 2.5 cm (12 in x 1 in). 'Stitch' along the edges of the strap in the same way as you did for the pockets, then lay the strap over the top of the bag (*fig 7*). Use a little water to secure the handle in place.

12 Finally, finish the board with two tiny golf clubs made by rolling about 5 g (⅛ oz) of black sugarpaste into a thin string for the handles. Cut this in half and stick onto the board. Make two tiny golf club heads out of a little brown and grey sugarpaste.

Decorating variation

Another easy sports theme is a sports cap cake. The cake itself was baked in an ovenproof pudding bowl which automatically gave it an authentic rounded shape. It was covered with sugarpaste and a semi-circle of blue sugarpaste was placed on the board to look like its peak. It could be decorated with models from virtually any sport or you could paint a badge or emblem to stick on the front using food colour.

Gingerbread

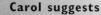

This cake is so easy to make. Once the gingerbread figures are baked, everyone can have a go at decorating them. If there's not enough room on the cake for them all, serve them individually as teatime biscuit treats!

1 Mix up and bake the gingerbread characters (see page 18 for recipe and details) and make at least two house shapes just in case one goes wrong or accidentally gets eaten! When they're cool, decorate the gingerbread people as you wish. You could cut out sugarpaste clothes in a range of colours and stick them on with a little water.

Use buttercream to pipe squiggly hair or to "glue" on small sweets or cake decorations. You could even paint expressions with food colour. Let your creativity shine through (1). When finished, place to one side.

2 To tile the roof of the house, you will need both the pale and dark blue sugarpastes. Roll both shades out thinly and cut out discs using either a circle

Carol suggests

If you look in the "Home Baking" section at the supermarket, you should be able to find packs of "writing icing". These are small tubes of ready-to-use colours and are ideal for use on projects such as this.

cutter or a small lid. Scrunch and re-roll the leftover icing as necessary. Stick a line of discs along the bottom of the roof using a little water. Place a second line above them so that they overlap slightly (2). Continue right to the top, then trim any tiles as necessary.

Add sugarpaste rectangles and squares for the doors and windows and any other home decorating embellishments that take your fancy! When finished, place to one side.

INGREDIENTS

- Gingerbread characters (see page 18)
- 2 gingerbread house shapes (minimum)
- 30 g (1 oz) red sugarpaste (rolled fondant)
- 30 g (1 oz) green sugarpaste (rolled fondant)
- 1 quantity buttercream (see page 19)
- Small sweets, silver balls, icing, cake decorations etc for decorating gingerbread
- 30 g (1 oz) pale blue sugarpaste (rolled fondant)
- 30 g (1 oz) dark blue sugarpaste (rolled fondant)
- 20 cm (8 in) square sponge cake
- 1500 g (3 lb 6 oz) white sugarpaste (rolled fondant)
- 4 tbsp white royal icing (see page 20)

UTENSILS

- Gingerbread men/women cutters
- Templates for house shape (see page 142)
- Piping (decorating) bags (see page 26)
- Scissors
- Star nozzle (optional)
- Paintbrush
- Rolling pin
- Circle cutter or lid
- Small sharp knife
- Carving knife
- 25 cm (10 in) square cake board

Decorating variations

Here are Jemma, Belinda and Natalie's decorated gingerbreads. As you can see, the scope for creativity is endless and you can never be too young to decorate gingerbread!

If you're pushed for time, or simply prefer a more traditional approach, you could choose the more conventional raisin and glacé (candied) cherry attire!

3 To prepare the cake itself, begin by carving it into a slightly irregular shape by cutting out a few shallow dips and hollows. Slice the cake in half horizontally and fill with buttercream. Reassemble the cake and place in position on the cake board, slightly towards the rear. Spread a thin layer of buttercream over the top and sides of the cake and dab a little water onto the exposed cake board around the base of the cake.

4 Knead 900 g (2 lb) white sugarpaste until pliable. Roll it out to a width of about 33 cm (13 in) and lift and lay over the cake and board.

Starting from the middle of the cake, smooth and press the icing carefully into position. Trim and neaten the edges around the board, and reserve any offcuts from around the board for use later.

Carol suggests

Don't worry about any cracks or bits of exposed cake board as these can be hidden by icing "boulders" later!

5 To provide hidden support for the house, place a lump of about 90 g (3 oz) white sugarpaste in a rectangular shape towards the back of the cake. Pipe

Carol suggests

If you make your gingerbread more than a day in advance, or if there's a lot of humidity or moisture in the air (common in kitchens), you may find that your gingerbread has softened and gone a bit "bendy". If so, place on a baking tray and re-bake undecorated on a low heat for 5-10 minutes.

a line of royal icing along the front and carefully stand the house in position (3). Make sure it stands securely. If it starts to lean forwards, place a few white icing "boulders" in front of it.

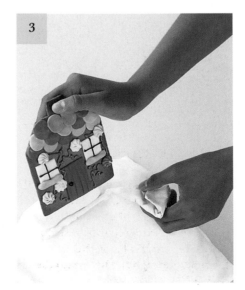

6 Place about a tablespoon of white royal icing into a piping bag, preferably fitted with a star nozzle, and pipe either a "snail trail" or a line of dots around the outside of the house (see page 27 for notes on piping).

If you don't possess a star nozzle, place the royal icing directly into the bag and snip a tiny triangle off the end.

7 Make a path from the front door by sticking about seven blue sugarpaste discs in a wavy line towards the front of the cake. Stick the two smaller characters in front of the house. Keep them standing upright with the aid of a large sugarpaste "boulder" and a dab of royal icing. Stick the two largest characters at the front against the side of the actual cake itself.

8 Finally, fill any gaps or cover any marks on the white sugarpaste with icing "boulders". Stick small sweets over and around the cake with royal icing for extra decoration.

Candles

Insert your candles into the white sugarpaste "boulders" around the cake. Add more as necessary, ensuring all are kept well away from the gingerbread.

An ugly green-faced witch and her big bubbling cauldron full of jelly snakes, eyeballs, spiders and other revolting things. What could be more horrible than that?

1 This is one of those rare occasions where if your cake rose enthusiastically in the oven it is actually a good thing. To make the cake into a cauldron shape, carve away any cracked, crusty bits (but try to retain a fairly rounded look). It is up to you which way you use the cake. Look at it both upside-down and the right way up to see which way looks the most cauldron-like.

If your pudding bowl cake came out of the oven looking pretty flat and level on top, it is probably best to use it upside-down with the widest part forming the base.

2 Slice the cake twice horizontally and fill the layers with buttercream. Reassemble the cake and position towards the rear of the cake board. Spread a thin covering of buttercream over the outside of the cake.

3 Dust your worksurface with icing sugar and knead 500 g (1lb 2 oz) black sugarpaste until pliable. Roll out and place over the cake. Smooth it into position. You should be able to lift and gently pull and fan out any sections that are tending to fall into pleats. If you have problems with awkward folds or cracks, just smooth out as best as you can and remember to cover with "flames" later.

4 Trim and keep the excess black icing from around the base. Out of this, roll 90 g (3 oz) into a long sausage. Paint a ring of water on top of the cake and lay the sausage in a circle to form the neck of the cauldron.

5 Make a handle by rolling 15 g (½ oz) grey sugarpaste into a thinnish string. Stick this onto the front of the cauldron, in a curve. Roll two 5 g (⅛ oz) balls of grey sugarpaste into balls and squash them both into discs. Press a circle into each one with a lid or piping nozzle, and a small hollow in the centre with the end of a paintbrush. Stick one on either end of the handle.

Carol suggests

Don't worry about icing sugar marks on the black icing at this stage, these will be dealt with at the end.

6 Thinly roll out 90 g (3 oz) yellow sugarpaste for the flames. Holding your knife almost vertical and just using the tip, cut out a very simple leaf shape. You can use the leaf templates (page 141) or cut these basic shapes freehand. Cut out as many as you can and stick around the base of the cauldron (1). Re-roll the icing as necessary.

7 To make the witch, first roll 30 g (1 oz) purple sugarpaste into a flattish conical shape to form the top of her body (2). Stick this onto the back of the cauldron, so that it rests on the bowl and uses the neck of the cauldron for support. For extra security, insert a couple of strands of raw, dried spaghetti through the body into the cake below.

INGREDIENTS

- 1 pudding bowl cake (see page 15)
- 1 quantity buttercream (see page 19)
- Icing (confectioners') sugar for rolling out
- 1500 g (3 lb 6 oz) black sugarpaste (rolled fondant)
- 30 g (1 oz) grey sugarpaste (rolled fondant)
- 90 g (3 oz) yellow sugarpaste (rolled fondant)
- 45 g (1½ oz) purple sugarpaste (rolled fondant)
- 2 strands raw, dried spaghetti
- 45 g (1½ oz) green sugarpaste (rolled fondant)
- 45 g (1½ oz) white sugarpaste (rolled fondant)
- Black, red, orange and green food colour pastes
- 1 breadstick
- 90 g (3 oz) blue sugarpaste (rolled fondant)
- 5 g (⅛ oz) red sugarpaste (rolled fondant)
- 2 tbsp royal icing (optional) (see page 20)
- 10 chocolate flakes or finger biscuits (cookies)
- 1 green-coloured fairy cake
- 30 g (1 oz) desiccated (shredded) coconut

UTENSILS

- Carving knife
- Palette knife (metal spatula)
- 25 cm (10 in) round cake board
- Small sharp knife
- Lid or piping nozzle
- Paintbrush
- Templates for and cloak (see page 142)
- Drinking straw
- Pastry brush

8 For her head, roll 30 g (1 oz) green sugarpaste into an upside-down tear shape. Stick this onto the body so that her chin (the thinnest part) rests on her chest. Check that it all sits securely.

Squeeze two tiny balls of white sugarpaste into "lemon" shapes, then squash and flatten to make her eyes. Stick onto her face. Make her eyebrows by rolling two tiny bits of green sugarpaste into little strings then bending them into "S" shapes. Stick one over each eye.

Add a tiny bent triangle of green icing for her nose and two either side of her head for her ears. Paint in the pupils with black food colour and add a mouth and a few dots for her whiskers!

9 To make the hair, roll out a tiny piece of leftover yellow sugarpaste and press a few lines down its length with the back of a knife. Cut out two long tapering triangles and stick one on either side of her head.

For the hat, roll about 5 g (⅛ oz) black sugarpaste into a cone. Tweak the tip into a wonky point and stick on top of her head. Roll a tiny piece of black sugarpaste into a sausage and stick around the base of the hat for a brim.

10 To make the arms, roll 5 g (⅛ oz) purple sugarpaste into a sausage and cut in half. Bend each of the halves slightly to form an elbow and stick into position against the body resting the wrists on the neck of the cauldron.

Place a 9 cm (3¼ in) section of breadstick into position. "Hold" it in place with two hands made from flattened green sugarpaste balls stuck at the ends of the arms and over the breadstick.

11 To make the cloak, roll out 90 g (3 oz) black sugarpaste. Cut out a tapering rectangle, using the template on page 96 if necessary. Stick the cloak around the back of the witch allowing the top edge to frame the face slightly to form a collar.

12 Make two eyeballs by rolling two 15 g (½ oz) lumps of white sugarpaste into balls and placing into the top of the cauldron (3). Paint two black pupils onto of the eyes and a few red ghoulish blood vessels.

Also, while you have the red food colour paste out, paint a red centre in the middle of each flame around the side of the cauldron.

13 To make the snake, use the blue sugarpaste and 10 g (¼ oz) black sugarpaste. Partially roll the two colours together to make a sort of blackish-blue woodgrain effect (see page 10). Roll the icing into a sausage, leaving one end slightly thicker than the other to form a head, and make a small cut into the base of the head for his mouth.

Arrange, drape and stick the snake down the side of the cauldron and onto the board. Stick two tiny white balls on top of his head for his eyes and paint two black food colour dots for the pupils. Make a tiny string of red sugarpaste for his tongue, sticking it from his mouth onto the board. Make a small cut and splay the end of the tongue.

Using a drinking straw held at an angle, press tiny "U" shapes all over the snake to give the impression of scales.

14 Brush away any icing sugar smudges around the sides of the cauldron with a large, damp (not soaking wet) brush such as a pastry brush. If it looks very shiny, leave to dry before putting the drips of "boiling liquid" down the sides of the cake or they will begin to dissolve.

15 To make the "boiling liquid" in the top of the cauldron, either water down a couple of tablespoons of royal icing to a spoonable consistency or mix 15 ml (2 tbsp) of water into 120 g (4 oz) icing sugar (add more sugar or water as necessary).

Stir in some orange food colour paste to the liquid and carefully spoon the icing into the top of the cauldron (4). Add a few artistic dribbles down the sides.

Carol suggests

If you don't want to make a green spider, hunt around your local sweet (candy) shop for jelly insects or snake sweets.

16 Arrange bits of chocolate flakes or biscuits around the base of cauldron to look like logs. You can "glue" them in place with a little buttercream. Place a green spider cake in front of the cauldron (see the Caterpillar cake on page 102 for cupcake recipe, then attach liquorice legs and sugarpaste eyes).

Take 30 g (1 oz) desiccated coconut and colour it green (see page 20) Spoon the "grass" around the base of the cake.

Candles

You should have enough room at the front of the board to position some sugarpaste "pebble" candle holders well away from the main cake. See page 27 for instructions.

Party animal

Here's a party animal who's almost completely partied out! If you're sure that they won't take offence, change the hair colour to match that of the recipient and substitute their favourite tipple for the beer can.

INGREDIENTS

- 1 pudding bowl cake (see page 15)
- 1 quantity buttercream (see page 19)
- Icing (confectioners') sugar for rolling out
- 320 g (11 oz) white sugarpaste (rolled fondant)
- 300 g (10½ oz) pale blue sugarpaste (rolled fondant)
- 90 g (3 oz) black sugarpaste (rolled fondant)
- 300 g (10½ oz) flesh-coloured sugarpaste (rolled fondant)
- 5 g (⅛ oz) dark blue sugarpaste (rolled fondant)
- 10 g (¼ oz) yellow sugarpaste (rolled fondant)
- 40 g (1¾ oz) green sugarpaste (rolled fondant)
- 10 g (¼ oz) grey sugarpaste (rolled fondant)

UTENSILS

- Carving knife and small sharp knife
- 30 cm (12 in) round cake board
- Rolling pin and wooden spoon
- Water and paintbrush
- Piping nozzle

1 Check that the cake will sit flat on the cake board when it is turned upside down. If the cake rose slightly unevenly in the oven, you may need to slice a little away from the top. Place the cake towards the back of the board, rounded side uppermost, and slice and fill the centre with buttercream. Reassemble the cake and spread a layer of buttercream over the outside.

2 Dust the worksurface with icing sugar. Knead 100 g (3½ oz) of white sugarpaste until it becomes pliable. Roll it out, then place it so that it covers just over half of the cake. Smooth and trim the base.

3 Roll out 100 g (3½ oz) of the pale blue sugarpaste. Lift and position this so that it overlaps the white. Smooth it into position, and again trim and neaten the base.

4 For the legs, roll 200 g (7 oz) of blue sugarpaste into a thick sausage about 20 cm (8 in) long. Cut it in half. Moisten the board and place the legs into position.

5 Using 200 g (7 oz) of white sugarpaste, make the arms in the same way as the legs. Stick them in position, pointing them forwards towards the front of the board.

6 For the feet, divide a 60 g (2 oz) ball of black sugarpaste in two and roll each half into a chunky oval shape. Stick one to the end of each foot with water, positioning them in a pigeon-toed fashion *(fig 1)*. To add detail, press the back of a knife into the sole of each foot a few times.

7 For the hands, take 50 g (1 ¾ oz) of flesh-coloured sugarpaste and roll into a thick oval shape. Cut the oval in half and using the back of a knife, press four lines into the rounded ends to make fingers. Stick the hands in place. His right one should be flat on the board and his left one on its side and curved, to hold the beer can!

8 To make his face, roll 200 g (7 oz) of flesh-coloured sugarpaste into a ball. Flatten the ball into a rounded disc about 11 cm (41 in) in diameter. Moisten the side of the cake and the board in front of the cake with water and lay the disc into position.

9 Make his smile by drawing a line with the back of a knife. For his eyes, roll out 10 g (¼ oz) of white sugarpaste and cut out two small circles 2.5 cm (1 in) in diameter. Stick these on the face. Roll out 5 g (⅛ oz) of black sugarpaste and cut out two smaller discs. Stick the black circles onto the white *(fig 2)*. Complete by sticking on a flattened ball of white sugarpaste as a highlight.

10 For the eyelids, roll out 10 g (¼ oz) of flesh-coloured sugarpaste and cut a circle about 4.5 cm (1¾ in) in diameter. Cut the circle in two and stick one half over each eye to create a droopy-eyed expression.

11 Take a 20 g (¾ oz) ball of flesh-coloured sugarpaste and slightly flatten it. Stick it in the middle of the face to make his nose.

12 For his hair, roll 20 g (¾ oz) of black sugarpaste into a long thin strip. Press the back of a knife along the length of the strip, then moisten the top of the head with water and lay the strip in place.

13 For the ears, roll 20 g (¾ oz) of flesh-coloured sugarpaste into a ball. Flatten it and push the end of a wooden spoon into the centre to leave a hollow. Cut the circle in half and stick both ears onto the head.

14 For the hat, roll the dark blue sugarpaste into a triangle. Stick this at an angle on top of his head. Roll the yellow sugarpaste into thin strings and stick to the hat.

15 To make the can, roll the green sugarpaste into a sausage. Flatten both ends. Cut out two flat discs from grey sugarpaste the same size as the beer can. Sandwich the green between the two grey discs and stick a small triangle of black sugarpaste onto the top of the can. Place in position.

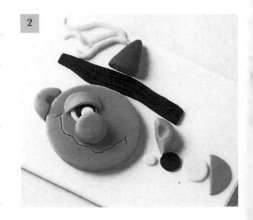

Twitcher

There's a type of person who at the mere rumour of a lesser-spotted swamp gurgler near Congleton will miss appointments, cross continents and sit for hours in freezing conditions just to catch the merest sight. Weird, but it makes for a good cake!

■ INGREDIENTS

- 1 pudding basin cake (see page 15)
- 1 quantity buttercream (see page 19)
- Icing (confectioners') sugar for rolling out
- 260 g (9 oz) black sugarpaste (rolled fondant)
- 20 g (¾ oz) pale blue sugarpaste (rolled fondant)
- 10 g (¼ oz) flesh-coloured sugarpaste (rolled fondant)
- 50 g (2 oz) brown sugarpaste (rolled fondant)
- 10 g (¼ oz) white sugarpaste (rolled fondant)
- Black food colour
- 150 g (5 oz) dark green sugarpaste (rolled fondant)
- 150 g (5 oz) mid-green sugarpaste (rolled fondant)
- 150 g (5 oz) pale green sugarpaste (rolled fondant)
- Brown food colour
- 10 g (¼ oz) pale brown sugarpaste (rolled fondant)
- 10 g (¼ oz) very dark brown sugarpaste (rolled fondant)
- 20 g (¾ oz) yellow sugarpaste (rolled fondant)
- 30 g (1 oz) golden brown sugarpaste (rolled fondant)
- 30 g (1 oz) green-coloured desiccated (shredded) coconut (see page 20)
- 30 g (1 oz) brown-coloured desiccated (shredded) coconut

■ UTENSILS

- Carving knife
- 25 cm (10 in) round cake board
- Palette knife (metal spatula)
- Rolling pin
- Water
- Medium and fine paintbrushes
- Small sharp knife
- Piping nozzle

1 Turn the cake upside down so that the widest part sits on the board. If it wobbles, cut a slice from the base so that it sits securely. Split it in half and fill the centre with buttercream and reassemble. Position the cake to the left of the board and then spread a layer of buttercream over the sides and top.

2 Dust the worksurface with icing sugar. Knead 250 g (9 oz) of black sugarpaste until it is pliable. Roll it out and place over the cake. Smooth it into position, and trim and neaten the base.

3 To make the twitcher, begin with his binoculars. Roll 5 g (⅛ oz) of black sugarpaste into a small sausage. Cut this in half and stick the two halves side by side, pointing outwards, on the front of the cake. If they start to droop at all, stick a little ledge of black sugarpaste underneath them to provide extra support.

   Next, roll 20 g (¾ oz) of pale blue sugarpaste into a sausage. Cut this in half and bend each half slightly into a curved boomerang shape. Stick these pieces onto the cake with the flat, cut ends up against the binoculars.

4 To make the twitcher's head, roll a 5 g (⅛ oz) lump of flesh-coloured sugarpaste into a semi-circular shape. Stick this just above the binoculars.

   Next, make two tiny flattened ovals of flesh-coloured sugarpaste for his hands and

stick these on top of the binoculars. Thinly roll out a little brown sugarpaste. Cut out and fringe a tiny rectangle. Stick this on top of his head *(fig 2)*.

   To make his ears, stick two tiny balls of flesh-coloured sugarpaste either side of his head and push the end of a paintbrush into each ear to add detail.

   Thinly roll out a little white sugarpaste and cut out two tiny discs (a piping nozzle is useful for doing this). Stick the white circles to the ends of the binoculars and paint a small picture of a bird with black food colour (you can miss this stage out if you wish).

5 Roll out a small piece of each of the green sugarpastes and cut out some basic leaf

Cut out a diamond shape for his beak. Bend it in half and stick onto the face. Stick two tiny flattened balls of white sugarpaste onto his face for his eyes and paint in pupils and eyebrows with black food colour.

Roll out and cut two longish triangles for his wings and stick these either side of his body in an outraged, hands-on-hips position. Carefully place the bird on top of the cake.

9 Moisten the cake board with a little water and carefully spoon the coloured coconut around the base of the cake to look like grass and earth.

TIP

If the person you are making this cake for 'twitches' for something else, substitute flowers or butterflies or a train for the bird.

shapes. Press a simple vein pattern into each one using the back of a knife. Starting from the base, stick the leaves around the sides of the cake, alternating the different shades and allowing them to overlap until the entire cake has been covered *(fig 3)*.

6 To make the tree stump, mould 40 g (1 ¾ oz) of brown sugarpaste into a rounded stump shape with a flat base and top *(fig 1)*. Holding the back of a knife vertically, press irregular lines around the sides of the stump. Paint a wash of watered-down brown food colour around the stump to pick out the bark.

Cut out a thin disc of pale brown sugarpaste and stick on top of the stump. Paint a few age rings on the top with brown food colour.

Roll some little bits of leftover green sugarpaste into thin strings and stick these up against the sides of the stump. Place it in position on the board and secure with a little water.

7 To make the smaller bird, roll about 5 g (⅛ oz) of very dark brown sugarpaste into a tapering sausage shape *(fig 1)*. Bend the head end up slightly and flatten and pull the tail into a point.

Add two tiny flattened balls of white sugarpaste for his eyes and a tiny triangle of yellow for a beak. Stick two tiny dark brown triangles either side of the body for wings. Paint the pupils on the eyes with black food colour.

8 For the large bird, use 30 g (1 oz) of golden brown sugarpaste. Mould this into a rounded cone. Bend the smaller end over to make a head *(fig 1)*.

Roll out a little yellow sugarpaste and cut out a rectangle for the tail. Cut a triangle out of one end and stick it against the back of the bird.

Bride and Groom

A special feature of this cake is that as the models are on a thin cake board, they can be lifted off and kept as mementoes. If you prefer a rich fruit cake instead of sponge, cover with a layer of marzipan first.

1 Level the top of the cake, spread with buttercream and cover both the cake and board with 700 g (1 lb 9 oz) of cream-coloured sugarpaste as described in step 2 of the christening cake on page 98. Place the cake to one side.

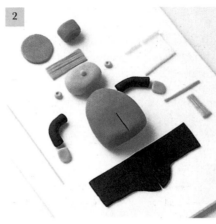

2 Cover the thin 15 cm (6 in) round cake board with 60 g (2 oz) of cream-coloured sugarpaste as described on page 16. Trim and neaten the edges. Place this to one side too.

3 On a spare board or worksurface, make the groom. Roll 80 g (2¾ oz) of grey sugarpaste into a chunky conical shape about 7 cm (2¼ in) tall. Check that the base is flat so that it stands upright. To add extra internal support, insert a strand of dried spaghetti into the body, leaving about 4 cm (1½ in) protruding out of the top *(fig 1)*.

4 Roll 15 g (½ oz) of flesh-coloured sugarpaste into an oval shape *(fig 2)*. Stick onto the body (use a little water as well), leaving about 1 cm (⅜ in) of spaghetti still protruding.

   Make his shirt by rolling out about 10 g (¼ oz) of white sugarpaste and cutting out a rectangle, using the template if necessary. Make a little cut in the centre of the top edge. Stick this to the front of the body, allowing the collar to just overlap the face.

Bend the collar forwards slightly.

5 To make the cravat, roll a tiny piece of pink sugarpaste into a thin string. Stick this just under the collar. Roll out a little more pink and cut into a thin, tapering rectangular shape. Press lines down the length of the strip using the back of a knife. Stick this in place on the front of the shirt *(fig 3)*.

6 Roll out a tiny strip of brown sugarpaste.

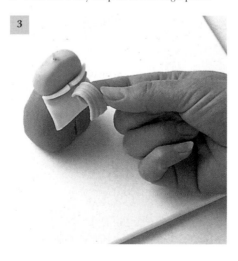

Cut out a thinnish rectangle and press lines down its length. Moisten the top of the head and lay this across for his hair. Stick three tiny balls of flesh-coloured sugarpaste

■ INGREDIENTS

- 20 cm (8 in) round sponge cake
- 1 quantity buttercream (see page 19)
- Icing (confectioners') sugar for rolling out
- 800 g (1 lb 12 oz) cream-coloured sugarpaste (rolled fondant)
- 90 g (3 oz) grey sugarpaste (rolled fondant)
- 2 strands raw dried spaghetti
- 30 g (1 oz) flesh-coloured sugarpaste (rolled fondant)
- 150 g (5 oz) white sugarpaste (rolled fondant)
- 10 g (¼ oz) pink sugarpaste (rolled fondant)
- 5 g (⅛ oz) brown sugarpaste (rolled fondant)
- Black and gooseberry green food colour pastes
- 30 g (1 oz) black sugarpaste (rolled fondant)
- 5 g (⅛ oz) yellow sugarpaste (rolled fondant)
- 90 g (3 oz) green sugarpaste (rolled fondant)
- ½ quantity royal icing (see page 20)

■ UTENSILS

- Carving knife
- 25 cm (10 in) round cake board
- Rolling pin
- Cake smoother (optional)
- Small sharp knife
- 15 cm (6 in) round thin cake board
- Water
- Fine and medium paintbrushes
- Templates for shirt, jacket and veil (see page 142)
- 2 piping bags (see page 26)
- 150 cm (60 in) ivory ribbon

on the head for his ears and nose and push the end of a paintbrush into each ear to add detail. Paint his features with black food colour.

   To make the hat, roll out 10 g (¼ oz) of grey sugarpaste. Cut out a circle about 3.5 cm (1½ in) in diameter and stick onto the head. Re-knead the rest of the grey and mould into a rounded shape with a flat base and top. Stick onto the head and bend up the sides of the brim.

7 To make the jacket, roll out 20 g (¾ oz) of the black sugarpaste. Cut out a jacket shape, using the template if necessary. Make a cut for the tails and wrap and stick the jacket around the groom's body (any gaps in the tummy area will be hidden by his arm at a later stage). Place the groom to one side.

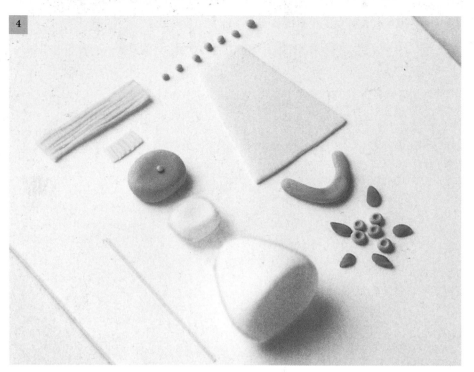

some on the bride's front to make a bouquet. Intersperse the flowers with tiny bits of green sugarpaste. Push little hollows in each flower with the end of a paintbrush.

11 Stick the bride and groom next to each other on the covered board and then make the groom's arms. Roll 10 g (¼ oz) of black sugarpaste into a sausage. Cut it in two. Bend one half into a right-angle and stick on the front of the groom. Position and stick the other one so that it looks as though the groom has his arm around the bride (fig 6).

 Add two flattened balls of flesh-coloured sugarpaste for the hands.

8 Make the bride's skirt by rolling 50 g (2 oz) of white sugarpaste into a pointed conical shape. Stick a 5 g (⅛ oz) oval of white sugarpaste on top (fig 1). Insert a strand of dried spaghetti as you did for the groom. Roll 5 g (⅛ oz) of flesh-coloured sugarpaste into a ball for her head (fig 4) and stick it to the body. Paint her features with black food colour and a fine brush and stick a tiny piece of flesh-coloured sugarpaste on the front of her face for a nose. Roll a little flesh-coloured icing into a thin sausage for her arms. Stick this onto the front of the body in a 'U' shape.

9 To make the hair, roll a little yellow sugarpaste into a thin strip about 6 cm

12 To make a rose, use about 10 g (¼ oz) of white or cream sugarpaste. Roll the icing into a thin strip. Paint a line of water down one side and roll up the icing (fig 7). Tweak the petals into position and slice a little away from the base so the rose can stand up. Make a total of at least eight roses in this way.

13 To make a bud, roll about 5 g (⅛ oz) of sugarpaste into a sausage with two pointed ends. Press a line down the top and bend it into an 'S' shape.

(2½ in) long. Press lines into it with a knife, then lay and stick it over the bride's head (fig 5). Tweak the ends up into a curl. Make a tiny yellow rectangle for a fringe. Press lines into this also and stick on her forehead.

10 To make her veil, roll out 15 g (½ oz) of white sugarpaste. Cut out a veil, using the template if necessary. Moisten the bride's head and back and stick it in place.

 Stick a line of tiny pink sugarpaste balls along the edge of the veil and one on the groom's jacket as a buttonhole. Also stick

14 For the leaves, roll out a little of the green sugarpaste and cut out a few very basic leaf shapes. Press a simple vein pattern into each one with the back of a knife and stick the roses, leaves and buds around the bride and groom. Add little swirls of green food colour and dots of royal icing, too, if you like.

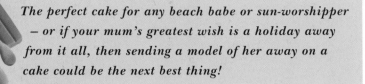

Sunbather

The perfect cake for any beach babe or sun-worshipper – or if your mum's greatest wish is a holiday away from it all, then sending a model of her away on a cake could be the next best thing!

INGREDIENTS

- 20 cm (8 in) round sponge cake
- 1 quantity buttercream (see page 19)
- Icing (confectioners') sugar for rolling out
- 500 g (1 lb 2 oz) white sugarpaste (rolled fondant)
- Blue food colour
- 150 g (5¼ oz) pink sugarpaste (rolled fondant)
- 30 g (1 oz) dark blue sugarpaste (rolled fondant)
- 40 g (1¼ oz) flesh-coloured sugarpaste (rolled fondant)
- 10 g (¼ oz) yellow sugarpaste (rolled fondant)
- 30 g (1 oz) brown sugarpaste (rolled fondant)
- 30 g (1 oz) green sugarpaste (rolled fondant)
- 15 ml (1 tbsp) white royal icing (optional)
- 50 g (2 oz) light golden brown sugar

UTENSILS

- 25 cm (10 in) round cake board
- Carving knife
- Small sharp knife
- Rolling pin
- Water and paintbrush
- Piping bag
- No. 3 nozzle

1 Level the top of the cake if necessary. Turn the cake upside down; slice and fill the centre with buttercream. Place on the centre of the cake board and spread a thin layer of buttercream on the top and sides.

2 Dust the worksurface with icing sugar and knead 500 g (1 lb 2 oz) of white sugarpaste until pliable. Partially knead in a little blue food colour for a marbled effect. Roll out, then cover the cake. Smooth the top and sides and trim any excess from the base.

3 For the air-bed, roll out the pink sugarpaste and cut out a rectangle 7 cm x 15 cm (2¾ in x 6 in). Using the back of a knife, press one line horizontally to mark the headrest, then press another five lines vertically down the length of the bed (fig 1). Lightly moisten the top of the cake with a little water and place the bed in position.

4 For the figure, take 30 g (1 oz) of dark blue sugarpaste and mould this into a conical shape. Pinch the middle to make a waist (fig 1) and stick on top of the air-bed.

5 For the head, roll a ball from 10 g (¼ oz) flesh-coloured sugarpaste. Take another 10 g (¼ oz) of flesh-coloured icing and roll this into a sausage for her arms. Divide this into two and flatten one end of each sausage slightly for the hands. Using 20 g (½ oz) of flesh-coloured icing for the legs, roll into a sausage, divide into two and flatten and shape the ends into feet. Stick the arms, legs and head into position.

6 Roll a small ball of brown sugarpaste out flat and cut out a thin strip for the hair. Press lines along the length of the strip with the back of a knife. For the sun hat, thinly roll out 10 g (¼ oz) of yellow sugarpaste and cut out a 5 cm (2 in) circle. Stick this over the face. Re-knead the leftover yellow and cut out a slightly thicker circle about 3 cm (1 in) in diameter. Stick this on top of the brim. Decorate with a few balls of pink icing.

7 For the palm trees, thinly roll out the brown sugarpaste and cut out about 14 small, curved tree trunks (fig 2). Press a few horizontal lines into each with the back of a knife and stick these to the sides of the cake. For the leaves, roll out the green sugarpaste and cut out about 28 basic leaf shapes. Make a few tiny cuts in each leaf. Bend each leaf slightly so that the cuts separate and stick a couple to each trunk.

8 For the waves, place 15 ml (1 tbsp) of royal icing into a piping bag fitted with a number 3 nozzle. Pipe a few lines around the air-bed. Using a damp paintbrush, pull the icing back from the air-bed (fig 3). Buttercream can be used as a softer, but yellower alternative. Stroke into place with a dry brush.

9 Finally, moisten the exposed cake board and spoon brown sugar around the base.

TIP

If you don't want to make up a full quantity of royal icing just for the waves, buy a tube of ready-made icing from the supermarket which comes with its own set of nozzles.

Stuffed elephant

Now here's a real party animal! Although I originally designed this cake for children, I rather suspect he will appeal to many adults as well as we have all felt how he looks at some time or another. If you wanted to dress him up a bit, you could attach a bow around his neck or place a few party streamers around the board.

INGREDIENTS

15 cm (6 in) round cake
1 quantity buttercream (see page 19)
350 (12 oz) pale blue sugarpaste (rolled fondant)
1.15 kg (2 lb 5 oz) pale pink sugarpaste (rolled fondant)
50 g (2 oz) white sugarpaste (rolled fondant)
20 g (¾ oz) black sugarpaste (rolled fondant)
10 g (¼ oz) dark pink sugarpaste (rolled fondant)
1 tbsp dark pink royal icing (see page 20)
Icing (confectioners') sugar, for rolling out
Water

UTENSILS

30 cm (12 in) round cake board
Carving knife
Small sharp knife
Palette knife (metal spatula)
Rolling pin
Cake smoothers
Wooden spoon
Fish slice (pancake turner)
Piping bag fitted with No 2 (round tip) nozzle
Paintbrush
Clingfilm (plastic wrap)

1 Lightly moisten the cake board with a little water. Roll out the pale blue sugarpaste and use this to cover the board (see page 16). Trim and neaten the edges and place the board to one side.

fig 1

2 Carve the cake into a rounded shape on a spare cake board or clean work surface. Slice it in half and fill the centre with buttercream. Spread buttercream around the sides and top as well and cover the cake using 500 g (1 lb 2 oz) of pale pink sugarpaste. Smooth and trim away any excess and lift the cake and place it towards the rear of the covered cake board using a fish slice. Be careful not to get any indents or fingerprints on the sugarpaste (*fig 1*).

3 Make a head using 300 g (11 oz) of pale pink icing. Mould it into a chunky tennis racquet sort of shape. Flatten the head slightly and pinch around the edge of the trunk to make a slight rim. Moisten the body and cake board and place the head into position. Press the end of a wooden spoon into the end of the trunk to make the nostrils and use the back of a knife to make a few creases across the top of the trunk.

4 Make four pink 50 g (2 oz) chunky carrot shapes for the legs and stick into position. Cut out four 2.5 cm (1 in) white circles and stick one to the pad of each foot.

5 Make two 50 g (2 oz) pale pink ovals for the ears and stick one either side of the head using a couple of scrunched up balls of clingfilm to support the backs of the ears whilst they are drying (*fig 2*). Cut out two smaller white ovals and stick these inside the ears.

6 Make a thin, tapering sausage (rope) shape for the tail out of 20 g (¾ oz) of pale pink sugarpaste.

7 For the eyes, cut out two 2.5 cm (1 in) round circles of white sugarpaste and stick these in place. Add two 2 cm (¾ in) black circles and finish with two tiny flattened balls of white as highlights.

8 Add two thin black sausage shapes as eyebrows and a fringe cut out of the dark pink sugarpaste.

9 Put the pink royal icing into a piping bag fitted with a No 2 piping nozzle and and pipe dots onto the board (*fig 3*).

fig 3

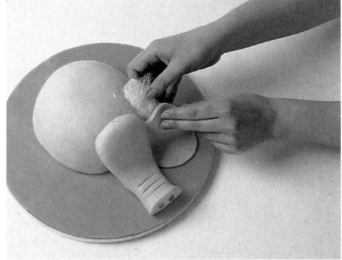

fig 2

TIP: *If you feel that piping all those spots would make you go 'dotty', substitute sweets (candies) instead.*

Fisherman

Fishing is apparently one of the most popular hobbies so there must be hundreds of wet and bedraggled fishermen sitting out there in the wind and the rain who would appreciate a cake like this when they get home. If it's the fisherman's birthday, the rocks double up as ideal candle holders.

INGREDIENTS

15 cm (6 in) round cake
1 quantity buttercream (see page 19)
550 g (1 lb 4 oz) brown sugarpaste (rolled fondant icing)
50 g (2 oz) black sugarpaste (rolled fondant icing)
40 g (1½ oz) flesh-coloured sugarpaste (rolled fondant icing)
185 g (6 oz) dark green sugarpaste (rolled fondant icing)
100 g (4 oz) white sugarpaste (rolled fondant icing)
50 g (2 oz) green sugarpaste (rolled fondant icing)
3 tbsp royal icing, (see page 20)
Green and blue food colours
Water
Icing (confectioners') sugar, for rolling out

UTENSILS

25 cm (10 in) round cake board
Carving knife
Small sharp knife
Palette knife (metal spatula)
Rolling pin
Cake smoothers
Cocktail stick (toothpick)
No 3 piping nozzle (round tip)
Sieve (strainer)
Small bowl
8 jelly (candy) fish
Needle and thread
Black boot cut out of a small piece of thin cardboard
Wooden skewer, trimmed to about 20 cm (8 in)

1 Carve the cake into shape (fig 1). Cut slopes into the sides and then cut a small semi-circle out of the side of the cake to make a bit of an inlet. Place the cut-out bits on top of the cake to make a hill.

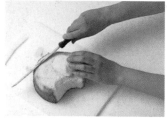

fig 1

2 Place the cake onto the board. Slice it in half, fill and cover with buttercream.

3 Roll out 500 g (1 lb 2 oz) of brown sugarpaste to a thickness of about 1 cm (½ in). Lift and cover the cake. Smooth the sides. Trim and keep the excess.

4 To make the fisherman's body, knead the remaining brown sugarpaste into a ball. Place it in position on the cake and secure with a little water.

5 To make the legs, take two 20 g (¾ oz) lumps of black sugarpaste and roll each one into a sausage about 7.5 cm (3 in) long. Bend the end of each leg into an 'L' shape to make the feet. Stick the legs into position. Insert a cocktail stick into the top of the body, leaving about 1 cm (½ in) protruding.

6 Roll 25 g (1 oz) flesh-coloured sugarpaste into a ball for the head. Moisten the neck and thread onto the stick.

7 Roll out 150 g (5 oz) dark green sugarpaste to a thick-

fig 2

ness of about 3 mm (⅛ in). Cut out a strip approximately 23 cm x 7.5 cm (9 in x 3 in). Moisten the body and wrap it round (fig 2). Press the tip of a No 3 piping nozzle (round tip) into the sugarpaste to make a line of buttons up the front of the coat. Make two sausages out of 10 g (¼ oz) of green sugarpaste for the arms. Stick into place. Add two small ovals of flesh-coloured sugarpaste for hands and

another ball for a nose and a strip of brown sugarpaste for the hair. Moisten the top of the head and stick a small flat 5 cm (2 in) circle onto it for a hat. Bend the front up slightly to make a peak.

8 Partially knead the remaining black sugarpaste into 50 g (2 oz) white. Mould the marbled sugarpaste into odd-sized balls for rocks.

9 Moisten the area of land behind the fisherman. Knead the green sugarpaste until pliable then push bits through a sieve to make some weeds. Cut off the strands and place into position.

10 Put 3 tbsp royal icing into a bowl and partially mix in a little green and blue food colours. Swirl the coloured icing around the cake board using a small palette knife to create the water and place the rocks and jelly fish into position (fig 3). Wipe round the edge of the board with a damp cloth.

11 Using a needle, thread the cotton through the top of the cardboard wellington boot and tie a knot. Tie the other end to the wooden skewer.

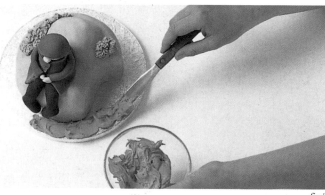

fig 3

12 Carefully insert the wooden skewer through the fisherman's lap and make sure that the wellington boot is positioned properly.

TIP: *A few strands of spaghetti can be used instead of a cocktail stick, inside the fisherman's body if preferred.*

Templates

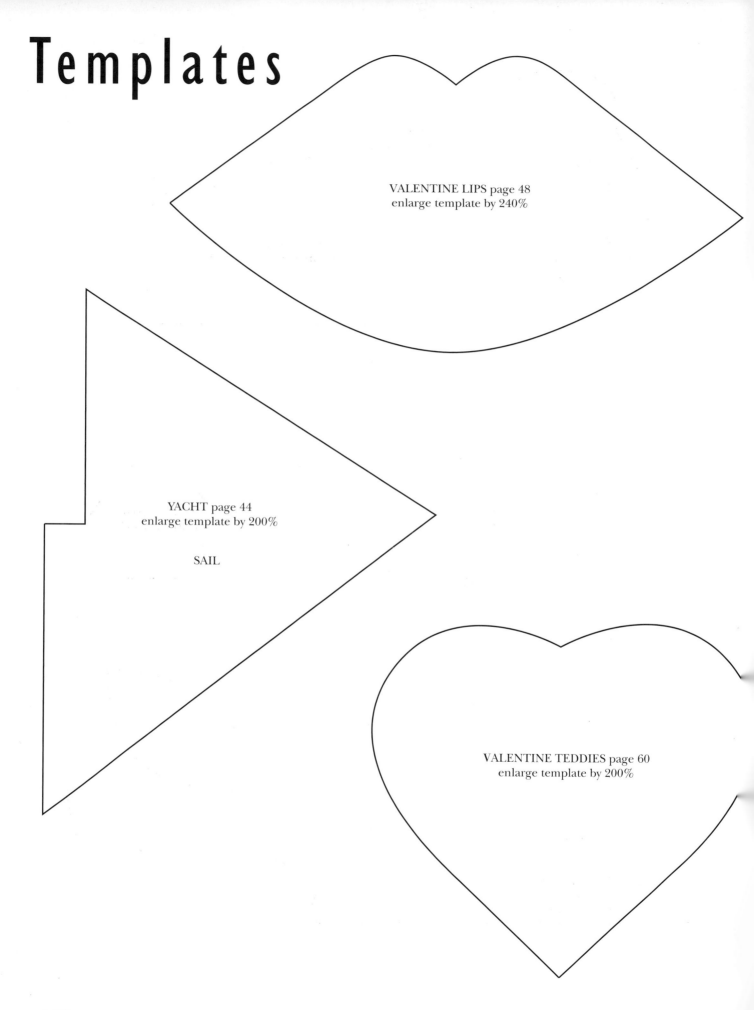

VALENTINE LIPS page 48
enlarge template by 240%

YACHT page 44
enlarge template by 200%

SAIL

VALENTINE TEDDIES page 60
enlarge template by 200%

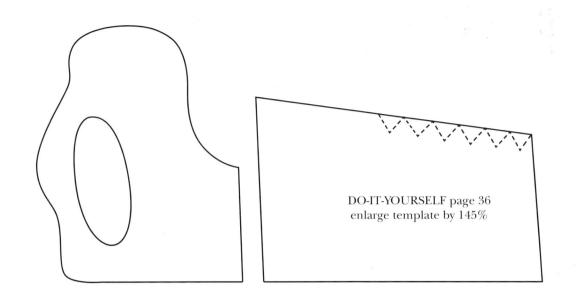

DO-IT-YOURSELF page 36
enlarge template by 145%

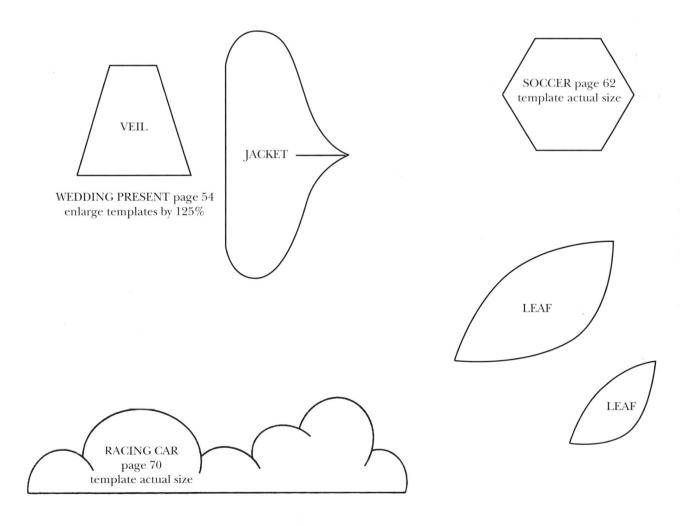

VEIL

JACKET

SOCCER page 62
template actual size

WEDDING PRESENT page 54
enlarge templates by 125%

LEAF

LEAF

RACING CAR
page 70
template actual size

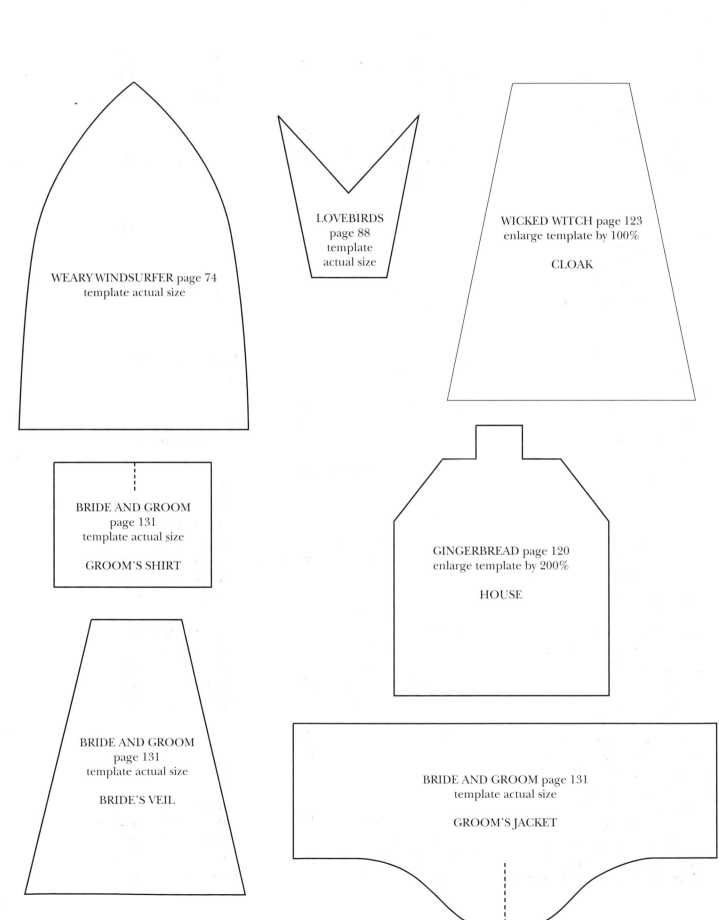

WEARY WINDSURFER page 74
template actual size

LOVEBIRDS
page 88
template
actual size

WICKED WITCH page 123
enlarge template by 100%

CLOAK

BRIDE AND GROOM
page 131
template actual size

GROOM'S SHIRT

GINGERBREAD page 120
enlarge template by 200%

HOUSE

BRIDE AND GROOM
page 131
template actual size

BRIDE'S VEIL

BRIDE AND GROOM page 131
template actual size

GROOM'S JACKET

Index